William George Aston

A Grammar of the Japanese Spoken Language

William George Aston

A Grammar of the Japanese Spoken Language

ISBN/EAN: 9783743394520

Manufactured in Europe, USA, Canada, Australia, Japa

Cover: Foto ©Paul-Georg Meister /pixelio.de

Manufactured and distributed by brebook publishing software (www.brebook.com)

William George Aston

A Grammar of the Japanese Spoken Language

A GRAMMAR

OF THE

JAPANESE SPOKEN LANGUAGE.

BY

W. G. ASTON, D. Lit.,

JAPANESE SECRETARY, H. B. M.'S LEGATION, TOKIO, JAPAN.

FOURTH EDITION.

𝔜𝔬𝔨𝔬𝔥𝔞𝔪𝔞 :
For Sale by Lane, Crawford & Co., Publishers.
Kelly & Walsh, Limited.

𝔗𝔬𝔨𝔦𝔬 :
The Hakubunsha.

𝔏𝔬𝔫𝔡𝔬𝔫 :
Trübner & Co., Ludgate Hill.

1888.

PREFACE

TO THE

FOURTH EDITION.

This Edition has been thoroughly rewritten. It is also much enlarged, and is almost completely a new work.

More exclusive attention has been paid in it to the Tokio dialect, which now bids fair to become the language of the upper classes of Japan generally.

At the suggestion of a friend, a literal interlinear translation of the examples has been added. No translation, however, has ordinarily been given of the particles which occur in them. Their meaning can be found in the chapter on particles.

The author takes this opportunity of acknowledging the assistance which he has derived from the writings of MR. E. M. SATOW and MR. B. H. CHAMBERLAIN. He is also indebted for some hints to DR. IMBRIE'S Japanese Etymology.

TOKIO, NOVEMBER, 1888.

TABLE OF CONTENTS.

    I. Syllabary—Pronunciation. 1
   II. Parts of speech. 5
  III. Noun. 7
  IV. Pronoun. 11
    V. Numeral. 34
  VI. Verb. 42
 VII. Adjective. 93
VIII. Auxiliary words... 108
  IX. Particles. 118
    X. Adverbs, Conjunctions, Prepositions and Interjections. .. 157
  XI. English into Japanese. 161
 XII. Honorific and Humble forms. 166
XIII. Syntax. 182
XIV. Time, money, weights and measures... 186
 XV. Errors in speaking Japanese. 191
XVI. Extracts. 192
     Index. 207

A GRAMMAR

OF

THE

JAPANESE SPOKEN LANGUAGE.

CHAPTER I.

THE SYLLABARY—PRONUNCIATION.

§ 1. IN Japanese, every syllable is supposed to end in a vowel, and generally does so, e.g. *sa-yō de go-za-ri-ma-sŭ*. The exceptions occur mostly in foreign words, or are owing to contractions. There being no final consonants, the number of syllables is necessarily small, and is reckoned by the Japanese at forty-seven according to one arrangement, and by another, at fifty. There are, however, modifications of some of them, by which the number is increased to seventy-five.

There are in Japanese no means of writing separate letters as in European languages, and each syllable is therefore represented by a single character, *n* final, which has a character to itself, being an exception. But *n* is supposed to represent an older *mu*.

The following table shows the syllables of the Japanese language arranged according to what is called the *Go-jiu-on*, or fifty sounds.

JAPANESE SYLLABARY.

a	i	u	e	o
ka *ga*	ki *gi*	ku *gu*	ke *ge*	ko *go*
sa *za*	shi *ji*	su *zu*	se *ze*	so *zo*
ta *da*	chi *ji*	tsu *dzu*	te *de*	to *do*
na	ni	nu	ne	no
ha *ba* *pa*	hi *bi* *pi*	fu *bu* *pu*	he *be* *pe*	ho *bo* *po*
ma	mi	mu	me	mo
ya	i	yu	ye	yo
ra	ri	ru	re	ro
wa	i	u	ye	wo

It will be seen that there are a number of irregularities and repetitions in the above Table. These are owing to the circumstance that there are certain sounds which a Japanese cannot, or at any rate, does not pronounce. For *si*, he says *shi*, for *hu*, *fu*, for *yi*, *wi*, *wu* and *we*, *i*, *i*, *u* and *ye*, and so on. These irregularities play an important part in the conjugation of verbs, and ought therefore to be carefully noted.

§ 2. *a* is pronounced like *a* in fat, father.
  e ,,   ,, *ay* in say.
  i ,,   ,, *ee* in meet.
  o ,,   ,, *o* in more.
  u ,,   ,, *oo* in fool.

I and *u* are frequently almost inaudible. In such cases they have been written ĭ, ŭ. Thus, *shĭta*, 'below,' is pronounced very nearly *shta*; *tatsŭ*, 'a dragon,' almost *tats*. Long or double vowels are distinguished by a line drawn above them thus, ī, ō, ū. The distinction between ī and *i*, ō and *o*, ū and *u*, must be carefully attended to, as the meaning often depends upon it. *Kōshi* for instance means 'an ambassador,' while *koshi* means 'the loins.' *Sōtō* means 'suitable,' but *soto*, 'outside;' *kūki*, 'the atmosphere,' *kuki*, 'the stem of a plant.'

§ 3. The consonants are pronounced as in English, except *r*, *h*, *f*, *n*, *d*, *t*, and *g*, which differ somewhat from the corresponding English sounds. The true pronunciation of these letters must be learnt from a Japanese, but the following hints may be found useful.

R before *i* is the most difficult of Japanese sounds for a European to reproduce correctly. It is then pronounced nearly like *d*, except that the tip of the tongue touches the roof of the mouth farther back. Some Japanese make it nearly *j* in this position. Before other vowels the Japanese *r* more resembles the English sound. There is never anything in Japanese like the rough pronunciation given this letter in French and Italian. *R* is often omitted before *i* in the words *gozaimasŭ, nasaimasŭ,* for *gozarimasŭ, nasarimasŭ.*

H and *f* are considered the same letter in Japanese and their pronunciation is not very different. The under lip does not touch the teeth in pronouncing *f*; it only approaches them as in pronouncing *wh* in *which*. In the vulgar Tokio dialect the syllable *hi* is undistinguishable from *shi.*

In pronouncing the Japanese *d* and *t* the tip of the tongue is pressed forward against the teeth instead of only touching the gum as in English. Little or no distinction is made by most Japanese between *dzu* and *zu.*

G at the beginning of a word is pronounced like the English *g* hard; in any other position like the German (not the English) *ng* in 'finger.'

In the syllable *ye* the *y* is in most words silent, or nearly so, and is often omitted in romanized Japanese.

In the case of double consonants, both must be sounded. Thus *amma,* 'a shampooer,' must be pronounced differently from *ama,* a 'fisherwoman;' *katta,* 'bought,' from *kata,* 'side.'

§4. The *nigori.*

The syllables *ga, gi, gu, ge, go, za, ji, zu, ze, zo* etc., printed in small italic type in the above table, all begin with soft consonants and are considered by the Japanese not as different syllables but simply as modifications of the syllables beginning with hard consonants in the lines immediately above them. This distinction is indicated in writing by a small mark, which is often omitted. *Ka* for instance with a diacritic mark is read *ga, shi, ji* and so on.

The formation of compounds and derivatives is often accompanied by the modification of a hard into the corresponding soft consonant, so that it is important to take note of this change, which, with the mark by which it is indicated, is called in Japanese *nigori,* or 'impurity.'

CHAPTER II.

PARTS OF SPEECH.

§ 5. The words 'Noun,' 'Adjective' and 'Verb' have two meanings in ordinary grammars of European languages. The term 'noun' is sometimes applied to a class of words inflected in a particular way, with cases and number, and it also means anything capable of being made the subject of a proposition. In other words it means one thing for etymological purposes and another in syntax, one thing in respect to changes within itself, another in its relations to other words. 'Verb' and 'Adjective' have double significations of a similar kind. This mode of classifying words according to two distinct principles viz. (1) the form of inflection and (2) their syntactical relations, is not without inconvenience even in European grammars, where it has led to the introduction of the awkward term 'participle,' meaning a word which is partly a verb and partly an adjective or noun. But such forms are after all the exception in European languages, where it is the general rule that words which as regards their declension or conjugation are nouns, adjectives or verbs are also nouns, adjectives or verbs for purposes of syntax. In Japanese, however, this is by no means the case. Here it is rather the rule than the exception that a word with or even without a change of inflection can be converted at pleasure into a verb, an adjective or a noun. *Iku*, 'to go,' for instance, looking to its conjugation is a verb, but if we consider its position in such sentences as *sugu ni iku*, 'he goes at once,' *iku ga yoroshi*, 'the going is good,' i.e. 'he had better go,' *iku hito ga aru*, 'a going person is,' i.e. 'there is somebody going,' it is only in the first case that it plays the part of a verb in the sentence, in the second it is a noun, and in the third an adjective.

The Japanese grammarians have avoided this ambiguity by classifying words as *na* or 'names,' i.e. 'uninflected words,' *kotoba* or *hataraki-kotoba*, 'words' or 'inflected words,' including the verb and adjective, and *teniwoha* or 'particles.' But this is not the place to attempt to introduce a more scientific English terminology. It will be sufficient to retain the familiar words, noun, verb and adjective, taking care to use them in such a way as to prevent confusion between these two significations.

§ 6. The noun is uninflected. All Chinese words in the Japanese language are uninflected, and are therefore strictly speaking nouns, but most of them, by the help of Japanese terminations are made to do duty as verbs, adjectives, or adverbs.

Along with the noun or uninflected word are classed the pronoun and numeral adjective, which in Japanese have no inflection. They have some peculiarities however which make it convenient to consider them separately.

There is no article. Prepositions and conjunctions are included mainly under the head of particles. Adverbs do not form a separate class of words. A particular form of the adjective does duty as an adverb, and other words which must be rendered as adverbs in English are in Japanese nouns, or parts of verbs.

The verb and adjective have a substantially similar mode of inflection in Japanese and should be considered as really forming only one part of speech.

CHAPTER III.

THE NOUN.

§ 7. In Japanese nouns have no inflections to distinguish masculine from feminine or neuter, singular from plural, or one case from another, but they are preceded or followed by particles which serve these and other purposes.

§ 8. *Gender.*—With the exception of a few common words such as *musŭko*, 'son;' *musŭme*, 'daughter;' *chichi*, 'father;' *haha*, 'mother,' no distinction is ordinarily made between the masculine and feminine. Thus *ushi* is either 'bull' or 'cow'; *mŭma* is either 'horse' or 'mare.'

When necessary, gender is distinguished by prefixing *o* or *on* for the masculine, *me* or *men* for the feminine. Thus *o ushi* is 'a bull;' *me ushi*, 'a cow;' *on dori*, 'a cock;' *men dori*, 'a hen.' These are really compound nouns. Such phrases as *otoko no ko*, 'a male child;' *onna no ko*, 'a female child' are also in use, *otoko* meaning 'man' and *onna* 'woman.'

§ 9. *Number.* As a general rule the plural is not distinguished from the singular, but a plural idea can be expressed whenever necessary by the addition of one of the particles *ra, gata, domo, tachi,* or *shiu*, which will be found more particularly described in Chapter IX.

NOUN.

Examples.

Yakunin gata.	Officials.
Ninsoku domo.	Coolies.
Kodomo ra or	
Kodomo shiu.	Children.
Neko domo.	Cats.

Some nouns have a kind of plural formed by reduplication. But these forms correspond rather to the noun preceded by 'every' than to the ordinary plural. Thus *shina* is 'an article,' *shina jina*, 'all sorts of articles;' *kuni*, 'a country,' *kuni guni*, 'every country;' *tokoro* 'a place,' *tokoro dokoro*, 'different places.' The first letter of the second half of these forms almost invariably takes the *nigori*. (See § 4.)

§ 10. *Case.* Properly speaking, Japanese nouns have no cases, but a declension can be made out for them by the help of certain particles, as follows:—

TORI, 'A BIRD.'

Nominative.	*Tori* or *tori ga*, a bird.
Genitive.	*Tori no* or *tori ga*, of a bird or a bird's.
Dative.	*Tori ni* or *tori ye*, to a bird.
Accusative.	*Tori* or *tori wo*, a bird.
Vocative.	*Tori* or *tori yo*, O bird!
Ablative.	*Tori kara* or *tori yori*, from a bird.
Locative.	*Tori ni*, at, to or in a bird.
Instrumental.	*Tori de*, with or by means of a bird.

The plural terminations come between these particles and the noun, as:

Yakunin gata ni menjō wo misemashita.
Official to passport showed

I showed my passport to the officials.

The student is referred to Chapter IX for an account of these particles.

§ 11. *Compound nouns.* Compound nouns are formed 1st—From two nouns. Ex. *Kazaguruma* 'a wind-mill,'

THE NOUN. 9

from *kaze*, 'wind,' and *kuruma*, 'a wheel;' *hanazono*, 'a flower-garden,' from *hana*, 'a flower,' and *sono*, 'a garden;' *kobune*, 'a boat,' from *ko*, 'a child,' 'something small,' and *fune*, 'a boat;' *honya*, 'a book-seller,' from *hon*, 'a book,' and *ya*, 'a house.'

2nd—From the stem of an adjective and a noun. Ex. *Akagane*, 'copper,' from *aka*, stem of *akai*, 'red,' and *kane*, 'metal;' *Nagasaki*, 'long cape,' the name of a place, from *naga*, stem of *nagai*, 'long,' and *saki* 'a cape.'

3rd—From a noun and the stem of a verb. Ex. *Monoshiri*, 'a learned man,' from *mono*, 'a thing,' and *shiri*, stem of *shiru*, 'to know'; *jibiki*, 'a dictionary,' from *ji*, 'a character,' and *hiki*, stem of *hiku*, 'to draw.'

4th—From the stem of a verb and a noun. Ex. *Urimono*, 'a thing for sale,' from *uri*, stem of *uru*, 'to sell,' and *mono*,' a thing.'

5th—From the stem of an adjective and the stem of a verb, as *Supensuru no maru-nomi*, 'a man who swallows Herbert Spencer whole,' where *maru* is the stem of *marui*, 'round,' and *nomi*, the stem of *nomu*, 'to swallow.'

6th—From two verbal stems, as *hikidashi*, 'a drawer,' (lit., 'a pull-out') from *hiki*, stem of *hiku*, 'to pull,' and *dashi*,' stem of *dasu*, 'to bring out;' *kigaye*, 'a change of clothing,' from *ki*, stem of *kiru*, 'to wear,' and *kaye*, stem of *kayeru*, 'to change.'

The first letter of the second part of a compound noun generally takes the *nigori*. (See § 4.) Thus the *k* of *kane* is changed into *g* in the compound *akagane*, the *f* of *fune* into *b* in *kobune*.

The final vowel of the first part of a compound is often modified, the most common change being from *e* to *a*. Thus from *sake*, 'Japanese rice-beer' and *te*, 'hand,' is formed *sakate*, 'drink money ;' from *shiro*, the stem of *shiroi*, 'white,' and *ke*, 'hair,' is formed *shiraga*, 'grey hairs.'

<small>The prefixes denoting gender and the honorific prefixes *o*, *mi* and *go* (for which see Chap. XII) must be considered as forming compounds with the nouns to which they belong.</small>

§ 12. *Derivative nouns.* Abstract nouns are formed from adjectives by adding *sa* to the stem, as *takasa* 'height' from *takai*, 'high.' It is occasionally added to words of Chinese derivation as *fubinsa*, 'pitiableness.' The adjective followed by *koto*, 'thing,' is also used in a nearly similar signification, as in the following examples. It denotes however rather the degree of a quality than the abstract quality itself.

<small>*Takasa wa iku-ken   desŭ ka?*   How many ken is it
height   how many ken is ?   in height?
Takai koto! dŭmo!
high thing   some how   What a height!
Ima no   wakasa   ni.   At your young time
present   youthfulness at   of life.</small>

Many nouns are simply the stems of verbs without any change of form, as *nokori*, 'remainder,' stem of *nokoru*, 'to be left over;' *kakushi*, 'pocket,' stem of *kakusu*, 'to conceal;' *watashi*, 'ferry,' stem of *watasu*, 'to make to cross over.' A few stems of adjectives are used in the same way, as *shiro*, 'white,' a dog's name, stem of *shiroi*, 'white.' There is here however a slight change of meaning, *nokori*, *kakushi*, *watashi*, and *shiro* having a more concrete signification than the verbs or adjective from which they are taken.

It will be seen later that for purposes of syntax, certain parts of the verb and adjective must be considered as nouns.

CHAPTER IV.

THE PRONOUN.

§ 13. *Watakŭshi*, 'I' (plural *watakŭshi domo*, 'we'), is the ordinary word for the pronoun of the first person. *Ore* (plural *orera*) is less respectful, and is the word mostly used by coolies, etc., to each other. To inferiors it is a somewhat haughty word. Students and soldiers say *boku* for 'I', *waga hai* for 'we'.

Temaye is a humble word for 'I,' much used by the lower classes of Tokio in addressing their superiors. It is also used as a pronoun of the second person. Some people use their surname instead of the personal pronoun of the first person.

Other words for 'I' are *watashi* (familiar), *watai* (by women), *washi* (very familiar), *wattchi* (rustic), *sessha* (formal), *oira* (familiar), *jibun* (properly 'self').

Examples.

v   *Watakŭshi wa zeikan no*   I am a customhouse officer.
      I   customhouse
   yakunin de gozarimasŭ.
   officer   am

v   *Ore mo ikō.*   I'll go too.
      I   too will go

   O yama no taishō ore   I'm the king of the castle. (in
   (hon.) mountain of general I   the children's game.)
   hitori.
   alone

Nanda ore ga yotteru   What! I drunk? Not a bit
what is   I   being drunk   of it.
(for *yotte iru*) *mono ka.*
               thing ?

Watakŭshi wa go dōyō   It is just the same with me.
I   (hon.) same
desŭ.
is

Watakŭshi wa sore wo suku   I like them, but I am afraid
I   them   like   they wont fit me.
keredomo, dōmo watakŭshi
although   somehow   me
ni wa aimasu mai.
to   fit (polite) will not

Watakŭshi wa Tekurada   I am Tekurada Futoshi. I have
I   the honour of meeting you for the
Futoshi de gozarimasŭ.   first time.
Hajimete o me ni
for the first time (hon.) eyes on
kakarimashĭta.
have hung

Sennen iro-iro go   In former times I was much
former year   all kinds (hon.)   indebted for your kindness.
kō-on ni adzukarimashĭta.
great favours   have experienced

Iye! watakŭshi koso.........   On the contrary, it was I who...
No,   I   (emph. part.)......

Ōkiku nattara   I too, when I grow big, intend
big   when I have become   to be a naval officer.
boku mo kaigun no shikan ni
I too   navy   officer
naru tsumori desŭ.
become intention is

§ 14. The personal pronoun of the second person differs according to the rank of the person addressed.

Anata, for *ano kata* 'that side,' (plur. *anata gata*) is properly a pronoun of the third person but like the German *Sie* has come to be used for the second. It is sometimes a noun as in the phrase *kono anata* 'this gentleman'. *Anata* is used when speaking to superiors or equals, or in fact, to any one who has a claim to be addressed with civility. *Omaye* (plural *omaye gata*) is familiar and condescending, and is the word used in addressing servants, workmen, the members of one's own family, etc. *Omaye san* is almost the same as *anata*, but more familiar, and is used chiefly by women. *Kisama* and *temaye* are used in addressing coolies and other persons of the lowest class in a familiar way. *Kimi* is much used among soldiers and students; *sensei* in addressing men of learning; a servant says *danna* (master), *danna-san* or *danna-sama* (rarely *anata*) in addressing his master.

Other words for 'you' are *konata* (for *kono kata*, 'this side'), *sonata*, (for *sono kata*, 'that side,' familiar) *sono hō* (by magistrates to prisoners or witnesses), *sochi* (to inferiors), *nushi* ('master', very contemptuous), *o nushi* (very familiar), *ware* (rustic), *unu* (abusive), *sokka* (formal). But *anata* and *omaye* will be found enough for most Europeans to trouble themselves with.

Examples.

Anata ni o hanashi mōshi-tai koto ga gozarimasŭ. you talk wish to thing there is	There is something I want to tell you.
Omaye koko ni matte ore. you here waiting remain	Do you wait here.
Kisama wa ore no uchi ni haitte, dō suru? you my house into entering how do	What do you mean, Sir, by coming into my house?
Danna no o mŭma no shita-ku wa yoroshiu gozarimasŭ. master's horse preparation good is	Your horse is ready, Sir.
Kimi wa doko ye iku ka. you where to go ?	Where are you going?

Boku wa gakkō ye kaeru I college to return *tokoro da.* place am	I am on the way back to college.
Ā! sensei wa Mina- you (lit. elder brother) *moto Kun de gozaimasŭ* Mr. (predicate) are *ka? Go kō-mei wa kane-* ? (hon.) high name previ- *te uketamawatte orimasŭ.* ously having heard I remain	Ah! are you Mr. Minamoto? I have already heard of your high reputation.
O nushi dachi.	You fellows!
Unu dorobō me.	You thief!
Unu uso wo tsuku falsehood stick *ze.* (emph. particle)	You are lying!
Ā! ii kokoromochi d'atta: ah good sensation was *Kisaburō kisama wa dō da?* you how is?	Ah! how pleasant that was! Kisaburo, will you have a turn? (Master, leaving bath, to servant.)

§ 15. The pronoun of the third person is *are* (plural *arera*). *Are* has no gender. It is often replaced for persons by the more polite form *ano hito*, 'that man' or 'that woman;' *ano o kata*, 'that gentleman' or 'lady' or *ano onna*, 'that woman.' These words add *gata* to form the plural.

Aitsu, aitsura are contemptuous equivalents for *are, arera*. *Kare* (plural *karera*) is sometimes used instead of *are* by educated people, but it belongs rather to the book language than to the colloquial. *Tō-nin* 'the person in question' is sometimes used for 'he.' *Ikken* is used when there is a sly emphasis on the pronoun, as '*Ikken ga kita,* '*He* has come.'

Examples.

Are wa mō Kōbe ni tsuki-mashitarō. already has probably arrived	He (she or it) has probably arrived in Kōbe by this time.
Ano hito wa junsa de gozarimasŭ. policeman is	He is a policeman.
Ano o kata Hiōgo no akindo ja nai ka? merchant is not?	Isn't he a Hiogo merchant?

§ 16. The above are by no means the only personal pronouns in use, but they will be found sufficient for most Europeans to know, and few persons will have occasion to use more than *watakŭshi*, *watakŭshidomo*, for the first person, *anata*, *anatagata* or *omaye*, *omayegata* for the second and *are*, *anohito* or *ano kata* for the third. The grammar of the pronouns is the same as that of nouns and they affix the particles in Chap. IX. in the same way as nouns. With the pronouns of the first and second person however the use of the plural particles when two or more persons are intended is the rule, instead of being the exception as it is in the case of nouns. A Japanese often says 'we' (*watakŭshidomo*, *waga hai*) for 'I.'

The use of personal pronouns is much more limited in Japanese than in English. They are not employed except in cases where their omission would cause ambiguity, or where there is an emphasis upon them. Thus, 'I am going to Tokio to-morrow,' will be *Miōnichi Tōkiō ye mairimasŭ*, except where it is doubtful whether the speaker refers to himself or to another person, when *watakŭshi* is added. If there is an emphasis on the pronoun, as in the phrase, 'I don't know what *you* may do, but *I* shall go to Tokio tomorrow,' it must not be omitted. Japanese generally prefer to indicate person by some of the honorific or humble modes of expression described in Chap. XII.

The indiscriminate use of pronouns is a very common fault committed by Europeans in speaking Japanese, and even disfigures some manuals of conversation which have been published. Not one personal pronoun is used in Japanese where there are ten in English.

§ 17. *Possessive Pronouns* are in Japanese nothing more than personal pronouns, with the addition of the possessive particle *no* or *ga*.

Examples.

Ano hito no iye wa   His house is a long way off.
that man's   house
yohodo tōi.
very much is far

Watakŭshi ga yubi wa itande   I have a pain in my finger.
my   finger   painful
iru.
is

Omaye no kiukin wa ikura?   What are your wages?
your   wages how much?

'Mine,' 'yours,' 'his,' 'hers,' 'theirs,' are in Japanese also *watakŭshi no, anata no, are no* etc., but they can easily be distinguished from 'my' 'your' etc. by the particles which accompany them or by the context.

Examples.

Kore wa anata no tsuye   Is not this your stick?
this   your   stick
de wa gozaima-
(sign of pred.)   is
senŭ ka?
not ?

Hei! Watakŭshi no desŭ. Yes mine is	Yes, it is mine.
Watakŭshi no da (for de aru) mine is to omotte machigaimashĭta. that thinking mistook	I mistook it for mine.
Watakŭshi no wa atarashiu mine new gozaimasŭ; anata no wa furū is your old gozaimasŭ.	Mine is new; yours is old.
Ano hito no de wa ikemasenŭ: his with can go not jibun no de nakute wa ki ni own without mind irimasenŭ. enter not	His won't do: I don't like any but my own.
Watakŭshi no wo o kashi mine (hon.) lend mōshimasŭ kara, go (humble word) became (hon.) yenrio naku —— ceremony without	I will lend you mine, so please don't hesitate (to use it.)
Anata gata no wa hitotsu ka your (plural) one or futatsu ga arimashĭta. two there were	There were one or two of yours.
Are no wo itadaite mo his having accepted even yoroshiu gozarimasŭ ka? good is it ?	May I accept his?
Taihen tamatta Great change collected nā! Kono uchi omaye no (exclam.) This among yours wa ikutsu bakari aru? how many amount are Temaye no wa sŭkoshi hoka I little other wa gozarimasenŭ. are not	What a tremendous lot have been collected! How many of these are yours? Mine are only a few.

§ 18 DEMONSTRATIVE AND INTERROGATIVE PRONOUNS.

This	That (2nd. person)	That (3rd. person)	That (3rd. pers.)	Who	Which	What
Ko or Ka (root)	So or Sa (root)	A (root)	Ka (root)	Da (root)	Do (root)	Na (root)
Kore (noun)	Sore (noun)	Are (noun)	Kare (noun)	Dare (noun)	Dore (noun)	Naui (noun)
Kono (adj.)	Sono (adj.)	Ano (adj.)	Kano (adj.)	Do (adj.)	Dono (adj.)	Nani (adj.)
Konata (pron.)	Sonata (pron.)	Anata (pron.)	...	DARE Ka	Donata (pron.)	Naki Ka
Koko here	Soko there	Asuko there	...	...	Doko where	...
Kochi here, hither	Sochi there, thither	Achi there, thither	...	...	Dochi where, whither	...
Konna this kind of	Sonna that kind of	Anna that kind of	...	...	Donna what kind of	...
Konnani (adv. of last)	Sonnani (adv. of last)	Annani (adv. of last)	...	...	Donnani (adv. of last)	...
Koitsu this fellow	Soitsu that fellow	Aitsu that fellow	Kyatsu that fellow	...	...	...
Kayō this manner	Sayō that manner	...	...	...	...	...
Kahodo this much	Sahodo that much	...	...	...	...	Nanihodo how much
Kaku or kō thus	Shika, so or sō so	Ā in that way, so	...	...	Dō how	Naze why

The above table gives along with the Demonstrative and Interrogative pronouns a number of words which it is convenient to consider at the same time, as being associated with them in meaning and derivation. Most of them are in very common use.

§ 19. *Ko, ka*, 'this.'

The root is only found in the compounds shown in the table, in *ko-toshi*, 'this year,' and perhaps one or two other words.

Kore (plural *korera*), *kono*. *Kore* is a noun meaning 'this thing,' or more rarely 'this person,' and corresponds to the French 'ceci,' *kono* an adjective equal to 'ce' 'cette' 'ces.' *Kore no* is also in use but with a different meaning from *kono*. *Kore no hako* for example would mean 'the box of this,' 'the box to which this belongs,' *kono hako* simply 'this box.' Similar distinctions are to be made between *sore, sono, sore no*, etc. *Kore wa, sore wa, are wa*, are often pronounced *korya, sorya, arya*, or even *korā, sorā, arā*, but it is better not to imitate these contractions.

Konata for *kono kata*, 'this side,' ought properly to be a pronoun of the first person and it is sometimes used for 'I,' but it is more common as a pronoun of the second person.

Koko, 'here.' The second *ko* means 'place.' It is found in a few other combinations as for instance *miyako* 'the capital,' lit. 'honourable-house-place.' The plural particle *ra* added to *koko, kochi*, gives them a vaguer signification. Thus *kokora* means 'hereabouts,' *kochira* 'hitherabouts,' 'somewhere in this direction.' In *sokora sochira* etc., *ra* has the same force.

Konna, konnani, 'this kind of,' 'in this kind of way.' *Konna* is for *kore naru*, 'being this,' *konnani* for *kore naru ni*, 'in being this.'

Koitsu 'this fellow,' is also used for inanimate things. It is for *ko-yatsu, yatsu* meaning 'fellow,' and is a very contemptuous word.

Kono yō ni, 'in this manner,' *kono yō na*, 'this kind of' have nearly the same meaning as *kayō, kayō na*, and are more common.

Kahodo 'this much.' *Kore hodo* is also in use in a nearly identical sense.

Kaku, kō 'thus.' *Kaku* is the older and book form but is still in use in certain phrases, such as *to mo kaku mo* 'even so, even thus,' i.e. 'howsoever,' 'at all events.'

Examples of *kore, kono,* etc.

Kore wa nani da?	What is this?
Kore wa teppō de gozaimasŭ. 　　　　　gun　　　is	This is a gun.
Kore wa ikura?	How much is this?
Kono ki.	This tree.
Kono tokei.	This watch.
Kono o kata.	This gentleman.
Kore wa Nihon go de nan' to this　　Japanese in, what *mōshimasŭ?* call	What do you call this in Japanese?
Anata ni kō iu shimpai you　to thus called anxiety *kakete　wa jitsu ni sumima-* having hung　truly　does *senŭ.* not finish	It is really inexcusable in me to have caused you such anxiety.
Boku wa kore de mo gakumon I　　this　even learning *wo shĭta　ningen　da.* done　human being am	I am after all a man who has gone through a course of learning.
Danna wa kochira de go- master　here abouts *zarimasŭ ka?* is　　?	Is the master anywhere hereabouts?
Kō　iu　　ba-ai thus called posture of affairs *da kara.* is because	Because this is the posture of affairs.
Korehodo osoroshĭkatta koto this much　afraid was　thing *wa gozarimasenŭ.* 　　is not	I never was so frightened in my life.

§ 20. *Sa* or *so* 'that.'

Sore, sono. There is the same distinction between *sore* and *sono* that there is between *kore* and *kono.* *Sore* stands alone, *sono* is joined to nouns. The remarks on the words in the first column of the table also apply to the corresponding words in this column and need not be repeated here.

Examples of *sore, sono* etc.

Sore wa kinodoku na koto de that sad thing *gozaimasŭ.* is	That is a sad thing.
Doko de sono kura wo o kai where that saddle buy *nasatta?* did	Where did you buy that saddle? ✓
Sonnara (for *sorenara*) *yoroshi.* if it be that it is good	In that case it is all right.
Sore ja (for *sore de wa*) *ikō.* in that case will go	Well then, let us go!
Sayō nara ikimashō. thus if it be will go	Well then! let us go! (more polite than last).
Sore ya kore ya de o ukagai that or this or for (hon.) call *mōshita no desŭ.* (humble word, past tense) is	I called on you partly for that, partly for this.
Sō to mo! Sō to mo! so that even	Yes! Yes!
Sonna (for *sore naru*) *mokuteki* that kind of object *nara yoshita hō ga ii.* if it is have given up side is better	If that is your object the best plan is to give it up.
Sore wa sō to. that thus	Let that be so—i.e. to change the subject.

Shite, 'having made,' is understood at the end of the last sentence.

Shō shō sokora (or *sokoira*) *de*   Wait a little thereabouts.
a little thereabouts
matte ore.
waiting remain

Yo no naka no koto wa mina   Such is the way of the world.
world interior thing all
sonna mono sa.
such thing (emph. part.)

Sō da sō yo.   So it would appear.
that is appearance

Sore ni sono toki hajimete   In addition to that, I then for
that to that time first   the first time learnt the truth.
hontō no koto wo shitta.
true thing learnt

Anata wa sō osshaimasŭ   You say so, Sir, but——
you so say
keredomo——
but

Sonnani o anji nasaru   There is no reason for your
so much (hon.) anxious do   being so anxious.
koto wa gozaimasenŭ.
thing there is not

Sahodo no koto de wa aru-   I thought it would not so very
so much of thing (pred.) will   much signify.
mai to omotta.
not be thought

Sa mo nakereba——   If that is not even so——
so even if is not

Sōshĭte (or *so shĭte*) *tsuide*   And won't you take the
thus having done opportunity   opportunity of buying me a
ni mikan wo sŭkoshi katte   few oranges?
at orange a little bought
kite kudasaimasenŭ ka?
come give (neg.) ?

Ai wa itasanakatta sō desŭ.   It seems they did not meet.
meet did not so is

Ame ga furi sō mo nai.   It does not seem likely to rain.
rain fall even is not

Fūfu ni natte   It seems they have become man
husband and wife having become   and wife.
iru sō na.
remain is

THE PRONOUN.   23

Sora! (for *sore wa*) *kisha ga*   There! the train is starting.
there!   the train
deru.
is starting

Sore   hodo   arimashite wa   What will you do with all that
that quantity   being   quantity?
dō suru?
how do

Dare ga sō iimashita?   Who said so?
who   so   said

Soko   ga kanjin   da.   That is the important point.
that place   important is

§ 21. *A* 'that.'

Are and *sore*, *ano* and *sono* must not be used indiscriminately. Just as *kore* may be called the demonstrative pronoun of the first person, *sore* is the demonstrative pronoun of the second and *are* of the third person. *Sore, sono* refer to something present before the speaker's eyes or to his mind; *are, ano* to something a little way off or not in sight. *Sore, sono* refer to the immediate subject of conversation; *are, ano* are used when a fresh subject is started. *Sono mūma* for instance means 'that horse' i.e. 'the horse you are riding,' or 'which you have bought,' or 'of which we are speaking;' *ano mūma*, 'the horse you rode yesterday,' etc. *Ano yo* 'that world' means 'the other world.' The phrase 'this that and the other' is a fair translation of *kore, sore, are.*

Kore, kono are the Italian *questo*; *sore, sono* are *cotesto* and *ano, are* are *quello.*

A Japanese often begins a sentence with an *ano* which has no meaning whatever and which merely serves to draw the attention of the person addressed.

The three words *konata* (for *kono kata*) 'this side,' *sonata* (for *sono kata*) 'that side,' and *anata* (for *ano kata* 'that side') should when used as pronouns mean respectively

'I,' 'you' and 'he,' 'she' or 'it,' but curiously enough they are all used in the second person, though *konata* may sometimes stand for 'I.' *Anata* for 'you' resembles the German use of *sie* 'they' as a pronoun of the second person.

Asŭko is irregularly formed. The regular form *ako* is in use in the western dialect.

Ayō and *ahodo* are not found; *ano yō*, *are hodo* are used instead.

Examples of *are*, *ano*, etc.

Are wa nan' da? that what is	What is that?
Ano daiku wa kita ka? that carpenter come?	Has that carpenter come?
Ara! (for *are wa*) *mata* there again *hajimatta. Anna* (for *are naru*) have begun such *kuchi no warui koto wo!* mouth bad thing	There! you are at it again. (Did any one ever hear) such bad language?
Omaye wa dō shite koko you how having done here *ni iru ka? Ano—watakŭshi ka?* are? I ?	How is it you are here? Eh! Ah! Is it I? (the use of *ano* here indicates embarrassment.)
Ano—Ikeda san.	I say! Mr. Ikeda.
Bakufu wa ano yō ni Shogunate that manner *natte kara.* having become after	Since the fall of the Shogunate.
Ā iu hanashi wa that way called story *mettani kikimasenŭ.* seldom hear	It is seldom we hear a story of that kind.
Ā iu fūzetsu wa ate ni report dependence *naranai.* do not become	One cannot depend on reports of that sort.

§ 22. *Ka,* 'that.'

The words in this column have the same meaning as the corresponding words in the previous one but they are much less commonly used and only by educated people. They belong properly to the book language. *Kano* has sometimes the meaning 'a certain.'

In some phrases *kare* is still in common use.

Examples.

Kare kore hiru desŭ. noon is	It is just about noon.
Kare kore iwazu to ike. not saying go	None of your objections, but be off with you.
Nanno (for *nani no*) *kanno* (for *kare no*) *to make- be beaten oshimi wo itta.* reluctance said	He went on talking as much as to say that he was not going to be beaten.
Hito wa kare kore to wa people that this *iwanai keredomo.* not say although	Though people do not make any remarks.
Nani ya ka ya.	Anything whatever.

§ 23. *Da,* 'who'.

Dare, 'who,' is the only word in this column, the places of the others being supplied by the derivatives of *do* 'which.'

Dare da? is	Who is it? who goes there?
Dare no mōsen?	Whose blanket?
Dare ni kane wo yatta? to money gave	To whom did he give the money?
Dare ga sō iimashita? who so said	Who said so?
Dare ka to omot- who (sign of indi- rect clause.) while *tara.* I thought	I wondered who it was.

§ 24. *Do,* 'which.'

Dore, 'which.' An old form of *dore* is *idzure* which is still in use in the sense 'at all events,' 'at any rate.' It is here put short for *idzure ni mo,* lit. 'in whichever (case).'

Donata, (for *dono kata,* 'which side'), is used as a polite substitute for *dare,* 'who.' A still more respectful phrase is *donata sama.*

From *dō,* 'how,' are formed *dōzo,* 'somehow or other,' *dōka,* 'somehow,' both of which words have nearly the force of our 'please.'

Examples of *dore,* etc.

Dore wa yoroshiu gozari-masŭ? which good is	Which do you prefer?
Dono fune?	Which ship?
Dono gurai yoroshiu gozari-masŭ? what quantity good is	How much do you require?
Dōka o negai mōshimasu. somehow (hon.) beg (humble word.)	Please do, I beg of you.
Dō iu hanashi de gozarimasu ka? how called talk (predicate) is ?	What is it all about?
Donata de gozaimasŭ? who is	Who is there? (polite.)
Donnani ureshi ka shiremasenŭ. how much joyful ? cannot know	I cannot tell you how delighted I am.
Dō shiyō? how shall do	What shall I do?
Dore! dore! kore desŭ ka? which which this is ?	Let me see! let me see! is it this one?

Doann yōsu ka to state of affairs ? omotte. thinking	Wondering what the state of affairs was.
Ima kokoro-atari wa nai ga, now mind hit is not *idzure tadzunete mimashō.* having inquired will see	At present I have nobody in view but at all events I will make inquiries.
Dō nasaimasŭ ? how do	What do you propose to do ?
Dō ka nasaimashīta ka ? somehow have done ?	Is anything the matter with you ?
Sono shōgun wa Napoleon that general *to dochi ga tsuyō gozaimasŭ ?* and which strong is	Which is the stronger—that general or Napoleon ?
Dō kangayete mo. how having thought even	No matter how I think over it.

§ 25. *Na*, 'what.'

Nani, 'what,' is used of inanimate objects only. There is no adjective form. *Nani no*, usually contracted into *nanno* or *dōno*, is used instead.

Naze, 'why,' is for *na-zo-ye*, *zo* being an emphatic and *ye* an exclamatory particle. See Chap. X.

Nanihodo, contracted into *nambo*, is used by the Japanese of the central and western provinces instead of the familiar *ikura*, 'how much,' of Tokio.

Examples of *nani* etc.

Nanda (for *nani de aru*) *?*	What is it ? or what is the matter ?
Kono mono wa nanda ? this thing what is	What is this thing ?
Sono gunkan wa nan' that man-of-war what *to iu ?* called	What is that man-of-war called ?

Nani shi ni   kita?   What have you come to do?
what do to have come   what has brought you here?

Nani? suguni muma wo hii-   What (nonsense)! lead the horse
what   at once horse having   here at once.
te koi.
led come

Nannara   (for *nani nareba*) Well then! as I have nothing
because it is what   to do, have you any objections
watakŭshi mo hima desŭ kara,   to my accompanying you?
  I   leisure is because
o   tomo   wo itashĭte-
(hon.) accompany having done
mo yoroshiu gozaimasŭ ka?
even good   is   ?

Nani shiro   issho   Suppose you go along with me.
what do(imperative) together
ni iki   nasai.
  go (polite imperative)

Bimbō da nan'to iu   kokoro   Putting away the feeling that I
poor   what called   heart   was poor or anything of that sort.
wo haishĭte.
  giving up

Yūbin-bato ni shi-komu to ka   Saying he was training it as a
post-pigeon as train   that?   carrier pigeon or something of
nani   to ka itte.   that sort.
something that? saying

Nanno go   yō desŭ ka?   What is your business?
what (hon.) business is   ?

Nani to ka   shiyō wa ari-   Is there nothing which can
            do manner   will   be done?
masumai ka
not be   ?

Naze hayaku konai?   Why don't you come quickly?
why quickly not come

Naze to iyeba.   To explain the reason why.
why   if say

Nani, in the combination *nan'desŭ* 'what is it' and similar phrases, is constantly introduced by some speakers in a meaningless way, something like our 'don't you know.'

§ 26. INDEFINITE PRONOUNS.—By the addition of the particles *ka, mo, demo, zo,* interrogative pronouns become indefinite pronouns.

Dare ka, 'somebody.'

Example.

Dare ka shĭta ni matte oru. Somebody is waiting below.
    below waiting remains

Dare mo, 'anybody,' is generally used with a negative verb.

Examples.

Dare mo shiranŭ. Nobody knows.

Dare   ye   mo   iwanai You don't tell anybody.
       to   even not say (imperative.)
yo.
(emph. part.)

Dare de mo means 'any one whatever.'

Example.

Dare de mo yoroshiu gozari- Anybody whatever will do.
            good   is
masŭ.

Dore mo, 'any one,' *dore de mo,* 'any one whatever,' are used in a similar way to *dare mo* and *dare de mo.*

Nani ka, 'something,' anything.'

Examples.

Kono hako no naka ni nani Is there anything in this box?
       box   inside
ka haitte   iru   ka?
 having entered is?

Kojiki ni nani ka o yari nasare. Give something to the beggar.
 beggar to   give   do

Nani mo, 'anything at all,' is used with negative verbs.

Example.

Nani mo gozarimasenŭ.   There is nothing at all.

Nanì de mo, 'anything whatever.'

Examples.

Kono musŭme wa nanì de mo taberu.
    this girl eats anything whatever.
    (Kono = this, musŭme = girl, taberu = eats)

This girl eats anything whatever.

Nani de mo shitte iru.   He knows every thing.

Nanì zo, usually contracted into *nanzo,* 'something or another,' 'any.'

Example.

Nanzo omoshiroi shimbun gozarimasenŭ ka?
    diverting news is not

Have you not some diverting news to tell me?

In the same way interrogative adverbs may become indefinite, as *doko* 'where,' *dokka* (for *doko ka*) 'somewhere,' *dokodemo* 'anywhere.'

Example.

Doko ka de mita yō ni omoimasŭ.
    seen manner think

I think I have seen (him) somewhere.

§ 27. REFLEXIVE PRONOUNS.—*Jibun,* 'self,' *jibun no,* 'one's own,' is the commonest reflexive pronoun in the Japanese spoken language. It is sometimes replaced by *jishin* or *onore.* *Waga* means 'one's own' in the phrases *waga ko,* 'one's own child,' *waga kiōdai,* 'one's own brothers and sisters,' *waga kuni,* 'one's own country,' and perhaps some others.

Examples of *jibun* etc.

Jibun de dekinai kara
can't because
tetsŭdatte kudasare.
lending hand give
Because I can't do it by myself, help me please.

Jibun ga warui.
himself is bad
It is his own fault.

Tegami wa yō ni tatanai;
letter use stands not
jishin ni itte o hanashi nasare.
going speak do
A letter is of no use; go and talk to the man himself.

Go jibun no toki de
(hon.) own time at
yoroshiu gozarimasŭ.
good it is
It will do at your own time.

Yokei na o sewa da:
needless (hon.) trouble it is
jibun no atama no hai wo oye.
own head flies drive off
I don't want your assistance; brush the flies from your own head.

Samukute, jibun no te da ka
being cold own hand is ?
nan'da ka wakaranŭ.
what is ? is not clear
It is so cold, I don't know whether they are my own hands or what they are.

Jibun no inochi wo sŭtete,
life abandoning
hĭto wo tasŭkemashĭta.
aided
Throwing away his own life, he aided others.

Observe the force of *hĭto* in this sentence.

For 'each other,' 'one another,' Japanese use the adverb *tagai ni* which means 'mutually.'

Examples.

Tagai ni mite orimashĭta.   They looked at one another.

Tagai ni tasŭkeru.   They assist each other.

§ 28. RELATIVE PRONOUNS—The Japanese language has no relative pronouns. To express the same idea, the verb of the relative clause is put before the word to which the relative pronoun refers. In the case of passive verbs a similar construction is found in English. Thus, for 'the man who was murdered,' we may say, 'the murdered man,' which corresponds exactly to the Japanese phrase, *korosareta hito.*

Examples.

Anata ga o uri nasatta jōkisen. sell did steamer	The steamer which you sold.
Sakujitsu katta hobune. yesterday bought sailing-ship	The sailing vessel which (we) bought yesterday.
Hayaku susumu fune. quick advance ship	A ship which sails fast, or a fast sailing ship.
Nihon go wakaranŭ hito. Japan language not understand man	A man who does not understand Japanese.

Instead of *koroshita hito,* 'the man who killed,' *korosareta hito,* 'the man who was killed,' it is possible to say *koroshita tokoro no hito, korosareta tokoro no hito, tokoro* meaning 'place,' but this construction can hardly be said to belong to the colloquial language. Such phrases, however, as *kiita tokoro ni yotte,* 'according to what I have heard,' are not unfrequent.

§ 29. OTHER PRONOMINAL WORDS:—

Hito 'man'. *Hito* is used in a similar way to the German *man,* the French *on,* and the English 'one' or 'people.' It may also mean 'other people.'

Examples.

Hito wo baka ni shite ikenai. people fool to making cannot go	You should not make fools of people.
Hito ga iu no ni. say in	According to what people say.

Hĭto no kodomo. children	Other people's children.

Mina, 'all,' is used either alone or after a noun.

Mina kareta.	They have all withered.
Ki ga mina kareta.	The trees have all withered.
Mina de ikutsŭ?	How many in all?
Mina san yoku irasshai- all Mr. well (hon.)come *mashĭta.* (past)	You are all welcome, Gentlemen.

Ika (root) 'how' is only found in a few combinations such as *ikani* or *ikaga,* 'how,' *ikahodo,* 'how much.'

Iku, 'what number,' appears in the following combinations—*ikutsŭ,* 'how many,' *ikura,* 'how much,' *ikumai,* 'how many flat objects,' *ikuhon,* 'how many cylindrical objects,' *ikuka,* 'how many days,' *ikutari* or *ikunin,* 'how many men,' and other similar phrases.

Itsu, 'when,' is found alone and in the combinations *itsuzo,* 'at some time or another,' *itsuka,* 'on some day or another,' *itsu mo* or *itsu demo,* 'at any time at all,' 'always.'

Riō-hō, lit. 'both sides,' is used for 'both,' but *dochira mo* is commoner.

CHAPTER V.

NUMERALS.

§ 30. The Japanese language has two series of numerals, one consisting of original Japanese words, the other borrowed from the Chinese. The Japanese series extends no further than the number ten, after which Chinese numerals only are used.

List of Numerals :—

	JAPANESE.	CHINESE.
1	Hitotsŭ.	Ichi.
2	Fŭtatsŭ.	Ni.
3	Mitsŭ.	San.
4	Yotsŭ.	Shi.
5	Itsutsŭ.	Go.
6	Mutsŭ.	Roku.
7	Nanatsŭ.	Shichi.
8	Yatsŭ.	Hachi.
9	Kokonotsŭ.	Ku.
10	Tō.	Jiu.
11		Jiu ichi.
12		Jiu ni.
20		Ni jiu.
21		Ni jiu ichi.
30		San jiu.
100		Hiaku.
200		Ni hiaku.
300		Sam biaku.
600		Rop piaku.
800		Hap piaku.
1,000		Sen.
10,000		Man.

Larger numbers are expressed by multiples of *man*. Ex. 150,000, *jiu go man*; a million, *hiaku man*. Consecutive numerals follow the same order as in English. Ex. 1868. *sen hap piaku rokujiu hachi*.

Riō 'both' is sometimes used instead of *ni* 'two' as in the phrase *riō san nin*, 'two or three persons.'

Nana jiu is sometimes used instead of *shichi jiu*, 'seventy,' in such phrases as *nana jissen* 'seventy cents.'

§ 31. The following rules are to be observed in the use of numerals:—

1. The only cases in which the Chinese numerals under eleven are employed are alone or before uncompounded or monosyllabic nouns of Chinese origin. Ex. *Jiu go kin,* 'fifteen catties;' *roku nin,* 'six men;' *hap piaku* (for *hachi hiaku*), 'eight hundred.' The letter changes which take place will be best understood from the numerous examples in § 32 and elsewhere.

2. The Japanese numerals when prefixed to nouns of Japanese origin lose the final syllable *tsŭ*.

Tsu is really an old possessive particle.

Examples.

Füta hako.	Two boxes.
Mi tsutsumi.	Three parcels.
Yo hiro.	Four fathoms.

3. The possessive particle *no* is sometimes introduced between the numeral and the noun. Ex. *Fütatsŭ no mono*, 'two things.'

4. The numeral is very often placed after the noun.

Examples.

Yama fŭtatsŭ.	Two mountains.
Mikan yotsŭ.	Four oranges.

5. The numeral may stand by itself.

Example.

Ikutsŭ aru?	How many are there?
Jiu ichi gozarimasŭ.	There are eleven.

§ 32. AUXILIARY NUMERALS. — It is comparatively seldom that the numeral is joined immediately to the noun. What may be called Auxiliary Numerals are much in use. They correspond to the English phrases, '*six head* of cattle,' '*four brace* of partridges,' '*two pair* of shoes.'

Examples.

Kami ichimai.	One sheet of paper.
Hakimono issoku (for *ichi soku*).	One pair of shoes.
Akindo jiu ichi nin.	Eleven merchants (*lit.* merchants—eleven men).

Most of these auxiliary numerals are of Chinese origin, and fall under Rule 1 of the preceding section. A few are Japanese words, and fall under Rule 2 as *kura hito tomai*, 'one godown.' They are commonly placed after the noun, but a construction similar to that described in Rule 3 is also admissible. Ex. *Sannin no akindo*, 'three merchants.'

These numerals are in daily use, and a knowledge of some of them is absolutely necessary.

NUMERALS.

The most common are:—

FOR ANIMALS.	FOR MEN.	FOR BIRDS.
Hiki.	*Nin.*	*Wa.*
1. *Ip piki.*	*Ichi nin* or *hĭtori.*	*Ichi wa.*
2. *Ni hiki.*	*Ni nin* or *fŭtari.*	*Ni wa.*
3. *Sam biki.*	*San nin.*	*Sam ba.*
4. *Shi hiki.*	*Yottari* or *yo* nin.*	*Shi wa.*
5. *Go hiki.*	*Go nin.*	*Go wa.*
6. *Rop piki.*	*Roku nin.*	*Roku wa.*
7. *Shichi hiki.*	*Shichi nin.*	*Shichi wa.*
8. *Hachi hiki.*	*Hachi nin.*	*Hachi wa.*
9. *Ku hiki.*	*Ku nin.*	*Ku wa.*
10. *Jip piki.*	*Jiu nin.*	*Jip pa.*
&c.	&c.	&c.

FOR LONG AND ROUND ARTICLES, SUCH AS BOTTLES, PENCILS, TREES, ETC.

Hon.

1. *Ip pon.* 2. *Ni hon.* 3. *Sam bon.* 4. *Shi hon.*
5. *Go hon.* 6. *Rop pon.* 7. *Shichi hon.* 8. *Hachi hon.*
9. *Ku hon.* 10. *Jip pon.* &c.

FOR BROAD FLAT OBJECTS, SUCH AS DOLLARS, SHEETS OF PAPER, CLOTHING, ETC.

Mai.

1. *Ichi mai.* 2. *Ni mai.* 3. *Sam mai.* 4. *Yo mai.*
5. *Go mai.* 6. *Roku mai.* 7. *Shichi mai* 8. *Hachi mai.*
9. *Ku mai.* 10. *Jiu mai.* &c.

---

* *Shi* is avoided in many combinations because it also means 'death,' a word of ill omen, and the Japanese numeral *yo* used instead before Chinese words.

NUMERALS.

	FOR HOUSES.	FOR SHIPS.	GLASSES OF WINE, CUPS OF TEA, ETC.	SHOES.
	Ken.	*Sō.*	*Hai.*	*Soku.*
1.	*Ik ken.*	*Is sō.*	*Ip pai.*	*Is soku.*
2.	*Ni ken.*	*Ni sō.*	*Ni hai.*	*Ni soku.*
3.	*San gen.*	*San zō.*	*Sam bai.*	*San zoku.*
4.	*Shi ken.*	*Shi sō.*	*Shi hai.*	*Shi soku.*
5.	*Go ken.*	*Go sō.*	*Go hai.*	*Go soku.*
6.	*Rok ken.*	*Roku sō.*	*Roku hai.*	*Roku soku.*
7.	*Shichi ken.*	*Shichi sō.*	*Shichi hai.*	*Shichi soku.*
8.	*Hachi ken.*	*Hachi sō.*	*Hachi hai.*	*Hachi soku.*
9.	*Ku ken.*	*Ku sō.*	*Ku hai.*	*Ku soku.*
10.	*Jik ken.*	*Jis sō.*	*Jip pai.*	*Jis soku.*
11.	*Jiu ik ken.*	&c.	&c.	&c.

FOR JINRIKISHA AND KAGO.

Chō or	*Dai.*
It chō	*Ichi dai.*
Ni chō	*Ni dai.*
San chō	*San dai.*
Shi chō	*Yo dai.*
Go chō	*Go dai.*
Roku chō	*Roku dai.*
Shichi chō	*Shichi dai.*
Hat chō	*Hachi dai.*
Ku chō	*Ku dai.*
Jit chō	*Jiu dai.*

For carriages the numeral is *ichi riō, ni riō* etc.; for books (vols.) *is satsu, ni satsu,* (copies) *ichi bu, ni bu* etc.; for mats, *ichi jō, ni jō* etc.

NUMERALS.

§ 33. ORDINAL NUMBERS.—The ordinals are formed by prefixing the word *dai* or affixing *ban* to the Chinese numerals.

1st.	*Dai ichi*	or	*Ichi ban.*
2nd.	*Dai ni*	,,	*Ni ban.*
3rd.	*Dai san*	,,	*Sam ban.*
4th.	*Dai shi*	,,	*Yo ban.*
5th.	*Dai go*	,,	*Go ban.*
	&c.		*&c.*

The ordinals precede the noun, the possessive particle *no* being introduced between.

Examples.

Dai ichi no yaku.   The first, or highest office.
Ni ban no fune.   The second ship.

Dai ichi, ichi ban mean literally 'number one.' *Me* i often added after *ban*, as *ni ban me no fune*, 'the second ship.'

§ 34. FRACTIONS.—Fractional quantities are expressed in the following manner: 21-100ths is *hiaku bun no ni jiu ichi*, (lit. of one hundred parts twenty one.) The *no* is commonly omitted, and *bu* substituted for *bun*. Thus for 'one third' the speaker has a choice between *sam bun no ichi* and *sam bu ichi*. When there is no denominator expressed, it is understood that tenths are meant.

Examples.

Hachi bu.   Eight tenths.

Shichi bu sam bu ni wake-   Divide it into seven tenths
                     having   and three tenths.
te   o kure.
divided   give

One half is *han*, or *ham bun*. One third and one fourth are sometimes *mitsŭ ichi* and *yotsŭ ichi*. These particular forms have been sanctioned by usage, but as a general rule Japanese and Chinese numerals cannot be combined in this way.

§ 35.   Examples of Numerals.

Sono kasa wa ikura? He; How much is that umbrella?
that umbrella how much One is fifty sen but if you buy
ippon   wa gojissen de gozari- three, I will make them one yen
one piece   fifty cents   is twenty sen.
masŭ ga; sambon   o   kai
          three pieces (hon.) buy
nasareba, ichi yen nijissen ni
if do   one   twenty cents to
itashimashō.
will make

Hito tsutsumi ni   hiaku   There are one hundred (dollars,
one   package in hundred   shirts, or other flat objects,) in
mai dzutsu   haitte   imasŭ. each package.
piece each having entered is

Sore wa fŭta tsŭki maye no That is a thing of two
that   two month before months ago.
koto da.
thing is

Mina   de ikutsŭ?   How many altogether?
altogether how many

Nanatsŭ gozarimasŭ.   There are seven.

Konnichi dora no   sōba Have you heard what the
to-day   dollar rate of ex- rate of exchange for dollars is
wo kiita   ka?   to-day?
change have heard ?

He, hiaku mai ni   hiaku Yes, it is 110 yen for 100
Yes, hundred piece in hundred dollars.
jiu yen de gozarimasŭ.
ten   are

Kore yori nan' ri hodo aru? How many *ri* is it from here?
this from what quantity is

Shichi hachi ri hoka (or *shika*)   It is not more than seven or
seven eight other   eight *ri*.
wa gozarimasenŭ.
   is not

Ni san gen.   Two or three houses.
two three houses

Shi go nichi.   Four or five days.

Nan' doki desŭ? or *Nan' ji*   What o'clock is it?
desŭ?

Kare kore yoji de gozarimasŭ.   It is just about four o'clock.
that this

Iku iro arimasŭ ka?   How many kinds are there?
how many colours are ?

Sōtai de kokono iro gozarimasŭ.   In all, there are nine kinds.
all in nine colours there are

Midzu wo hĭto kuchi kurero.   Give me a mouthful of water.
Water one mouth give

Hitotsŭ no samatage ga aru.   There is one obstacle.
one obstacle there is

Jiu-nin to-iro.   As many men, as many minds.
10 men 10 colour

CHAPTER VI.

THE VERB.

§ 36. The verb in Japanese has no means of expressing distinctions of number or, except indirectly, of person. *Kasu*, for instance, may mean, 'I lend,' 'thou lendest,' 'he lends,' 'we, you, or they lend,' according to circumstances.

In the spoken language there are two conjugations of verbs. The following table shows the terminations of the principal parts in each conjugation:—

	CONJ. I.	CONJ. II.
Stem...	*i*	*e* or *i*
Base for Negative and Future forms............	*a*	*e* or *i*
Present Indicative...........................	*u*	*eru* or *iru*
Base for Conditional forms	*e*	'*ere* or *ire*

It is not altogether arbitrarily that these conjugations have been termed the 'first' and the 'second.' The great majority of underived verbs are conjugated according to the first conjugation; all passive and most causative and other derivative verbs belong to the second.

§ 37. Table showing the formation of the principal parts in different verbs:—

	CONJUGATION I.							CONJUG. II.	
	lend	wait	be	write	pour	end	read	call	eat	can
Stem	*kashi*	*machi*	*ari*	*kaki*	*tsugi*	*shimai*	*yomi*	*yobi*	*tabe*	*deki*
Neg. Base...	*kasa*	*mata*	*ara*	*kaka*	*tsuga*	*shimawa*	*yoma*	*yoba*	*tabe*	*deki*
Pres. Indic..	*kasu*	*matsu*	*aru*	*kaku*	*tsugu*	*shimau*	*yomu*	*yobu*	*taberu*	*dekiru*
Con. Base...	*kase*	*mate*	*are*	*kake*	*tsuge*	*shimaye*	*yome*	*yobe*	*tabere*	*dekire*

THE VERB.   43

As the Japanese language does not possess the sounds *tu*, *ti* and *si*, *tsu*, *chi* and *shi* are substituted wherever they are required by the conjugation. This will explain several apparent irregularities in the above table.

The conjugation of *shimau* would be *shimawi*, *shimawa*, *shimawu*, *shimawe*, but, as is explained in § 1, *wi*, *wu* and *we* are unknown syllables in Japanese, being replaced by *i*, *u* and *ye*.

§ 38. To each of the principal parts of the verb, certain particles or terminations are annexed. In this way forms are produced in some degree similar to the moods and tenses of European grammars. These terminations are shown in the annexed tables.

It will be observed that in most cases they are merely tacked on to the verb without any change. This is what is called 'agglutination,' and owing to the prevalence of this method in Japanese it has been rightly called an agglutinative language. There are however several cases where something more than mere 'tacking on' has taken place. The future, *kasō*, which contains three elements, closely welded together, is an example. *Kasō* is for *kas*+*a*+*mu*, the root+sign of neg. base+future particle. *Matta*, the past tense of *matsu*, 'to wait,' is another case where the original elements have been so consolidated together as to be quite indistinguishable on a superficial examination. *Matta* is for *mach*+*i*+*te*+*ar*+*u*, i.e. the root+sign of stem+sign of participle+root of verb 'to be'+sign of indic. mood.

In some cases the terminations treated of in this chapter are really identical with particles described in Chapter IX.

Those readers who prefer the more old fashioned style of conjugation according to moods and tenses are referred to the table given at the end of this chapter, but they are recommended to master at least the principle of the formation of the various tenses before proceeding further.

44 THE VERB.

§ 39. CONJUGATION I.

Kasu, to lend.

Stem	*Kashi*, lend.
Past Participle	*Kashi-te*, having lent or lending.
Past Tense	,, *ta*, (he) lent or has lent.
Conditional of do. ..	,, *tareba*, if or when (he) lent, or has lent.
Hypothetical of do. ..	,, *taraba*, if (he) had lent.
Probable Past	,, *tarō*, (he) probably lent.
Alternative Form....	,, *tari*, at one time lending.
Concessive Past	,, *taredo*, though (he) lent.
Desiderative Adj.....	,, *tai*, (he) wishes to lend.
Polite Form	,, *masŭ*, (he) lends.
Negative Base	*Kasa*.
Neg. of Pres. Indic. ..	*Kasa nŭ*, (he) does not lend.
Negative Past	,, *nanda*, (he) did not lend.
Neg. Conditional	,, *neba*, if (he) does not lend.
Neg. Hypothetical ..	,, *zu ba*, if (he) were not to lend.
Neg. Concessive	,, *nedo*, though (he) does not lend.
Neg. Participle	,, *de* or *zu*, not lending.
Hypothetical	,, *ba*, if (he) were to lend.
Neg. Adjective	,, *nai*, (he) does not lend.
Future	*Kasō*, (he) will lend.
Present Indicative ...	*Kasu*, (he) lends.
Neg. Imperative	*Kasu na*, do not lend.
Neg. Future	,, *mai*, (he) will not lend.
Conditional Base	*Kase*.
Imperative	*Kase*, lend.
Conditional	,, *ba*, if (he) lend.
Concessive..........	;, *do*, though (he) lend.

§ 40.   CONJUGATION II.

Taberu, to eat.

Stem	*Tabe*, eat.
Past Participle	*Tabe te*, having eaten or eating.
Past Tense	„ *ta*, (he) ate.
Conditional of do. ..	„ *tareba*, if or when (he) ate, or has eaten.
Hypothetical of do. ..	„ *taraba*, if (he) had eaten.
Probable Past	„ *tarō*, (he) has probably eaten.
Alternative Form....	„ *tari*, at one time eating.
Concessive Past	„ *taredo*, though (he) ate.
Desiderative Adj.....	„ *tai*, (he) wishes to eat.
Polite Form	„ *masŭ*, (he) eats.
Imperative	„ *ro*, eat!
Negative Base	*Tabe*.
Neg. Pres. Indic.	*Tabe nŭ*, (he) does not eat.
Neg. Past Indic. .,..	„ *nanda*, (he) did not eat.
Neg. Conditional	„ *neba*, if (he) do not eat.
Neg. Hypothetical ..	„ *zuba*, if (he) were not to eat.
Neg. Concessive	„ *nedo*, though (he) does not eat.
Neg. Participle	„ *de* or *zu*, not eating.
Hypothetical	„ *ba*, if (he) were to eat.
Neg. Adjective	„ *nai*, (he) does not eat.
Neg. Future	„ *mai*, (he) will not eat.
Future	„ *yō*, (he) will eat.
Present Indicative ..	*Taberu*, (he) eats.
Neg. Imperative	*Taberu na*, do not eat.
Conditional Base	*Tabere*.
Conditional	*Tabere ba*, if (he) eat.
Concessive	„ *do*, though (he) eat.

§ 41. The following examples show the letter-changes which take place when the stems of verbs of the first conjugation ending in *chi, ri, ki, gi, i* preceded by a vowel, *mi* or *bi* come before the terminations *te, ta, tareba, tara, taraba, tarō, tari,* and *taredo*.

    Machi-te becomes *matte, machita matta,* etc.
    Ari-te   ,,   *atte.*
    Kaki-te   ,,   *kaite.*
    Tsugi-te.   ,,   *tsuide* or *tsuite.*
    Shimai-te   ,,   *shimatte.*
    Omoi-te   ,,   *omotte.*
    Yomi-te.   ,,   *yonde.*
    Yobi-te   ,,   *yonde.*

Exception :—*Iki-te* (*iku* 'to go') becomes *itte* not *iite.*

§ 42. IRREGULAR VERBS. *Kuru* 'to come,' *suru* 'to do' and the polite auxiliary *masŭ* are somewhat irregular. Their conjugation is given below.

For the future of *kuru, koyō* is best. *Kiyō,* which is also used, is not so good. *Kō* is sometimes heard in the phrase *itte kō ka,* 'having gone shall I come.'

Instead of *shō,* the future of *suru,* 'to do,' *seyō* is sometimes heard, and for the negative future *semai,* some people say *sumai* or *shimai.* But these forms are less correct than those given in the tables.

Masŭ has no desiderative form. Instead of *ikimashītai,* we must say *ikitō gozaimasŭ* 'I wish to go.' *Mase* (imperative) is often pronounced *mashi* by careless speakers. *Masuru* is more formal, and less common than *masŭ.*

Masŭ is not now in use as a separate word, but only combined with other verbs to form polite tenses.

THE VERB. 47.

§ 43. *Kuru*, to come.

Stem	*Ki*.	come.
Past Participle....	*Ki te*	coming or having come.
Past Tense	,, *ta*	(he) came, or (he) has come.
Conditional of do. ..	,, *tareba*	if or when (he) came.
Hypothetical of do.	,, *taraba*	if (he) had come.
Probable Past	,, *tarō*	(he) has probably come.
Alternative	,, *tari*	at one time coming.
Concessive of Past.	,, *taredo*	although (he) came.
Desiderative Adj. ..	,, *tai*	(he) wishes to come.
Polite Form	,, *masŭ*	(he) comes.
Negative Base	*Ko*	
Neg. of Pres. Indic.	*Ko nŭ*	(he) does not come.
Neg. of Past Indic.	,, *nanda*	(he) did not come.
Neg. of Conditional.	,, *neba*	if (he) does not come.
Neg. of Hypothet.	,, *zuba*	should (he) not come.
Neg. of Concessive.	,, *nedo*	though (he) do not come.
Neg. Participle	,, *de, zu*	not coming, or without coming.
Hypothetical	,, *ba*	should (he) come.
Neg. Adjective	,, *nai*	(he) does not come.
Neg. of Future	,, *mai*	(he) will not come.
Future............	*Kō* or *koyō*	(he) will come.
Imperative	*Koi*	come!
Present Indicative..	*Kuru*	(he) comes.
Neg. Imperative ..	*Kuru na*	do not come!
Conditional Base ..	*Kure*	
Conditional	*Kure-ba*	if (he) comes.
Concessive	,, *do*	though (he) comes.

§ 44. *Suru,* to do.

Stem	*Shi*	do.
Past Participle	*Shi te*	doing or having done.
Past Tense	,, *ta*	(he) did or has done.
Conditional of do. ..	,, *tareba*	if or since (he) did.
Hypothetical of do.	,, *taraba*	if (he) had done.
Probable Past	,, *tarō*	(he) probably did.
Alternative	,, *tari*	at one time doing.
Concessive Past ..	,, *taredo*	though (he) did.
Desiderative Adj. ..	,, *tai*	(he) wishes to do.
Polite Form	,, *masŭ*	(he) does.
Imperative	,, *ro*	do!
Neg. Adjective	,, *nai*	(he) does not or will not do.
Negative Base	*Se.*	———
Neg. of Pres. Indic.	*Se nŭ*	(he) does not do.
Neg. of Past Indic.	,, *nanda*	(he) did not.
Neg. of Conditional.	,, *neba*	if (he) does not.
Neg. of Hypothetical	,, *zuba*	should (he) not do.
Neg. of Concessive.	,, *nedo*	though (he) do not.
Neg. Participle	,, *de* or *zu*	not doing, or without doing.
Hypothetical	,, *ba*	should (he) do.
Neg. Future	,, *mai*	(he) will not do.
Future............	*Shō*	(he) will do.
Pres. Indicative....	*Suru*	(he) does.
Neg. Imperative ..	*Suru na*	do not!
Conditional Base ..	*Sure*	———
Conditional	*Sure ba*	if (he) does.
Concessive	,, *do*	though (he) does.

THE VERB.

§ 45. *Masŭ*, to be.

Stem	*Mashi*	be.
Past Participle	*Mashĭ te*	being or having been.
Past Tense	,, *ta*	(he) was or has been.
Conditional of do. ..	,, *tareba*	if or since (he) was.
Hypothetical of do.	,, *taraba*	if (he) had been.
Probable Past	,, *tarō*	(he) probably was.
Alternative	,, *tari*	at one time being.
Concessive Past ..	,, *taredo*	though (he) was.
Desiderative Adj. ..	Wanting	
Polite Form	Wanting	
Negative Base	*Mase*	
Neg. of Pres. Indic.	*Mase-nŭ*	(he) is not.
Neg. of Past Indic.	,, *nanda*	(he) was not.
Neg. of Conditional.	,, *neba*	if (he) is not.
Neg. of Hypothetical	,, *zuba*	should (he) not be.
Neg. of Concessive.	,, *nedo*	though (he) is not.
Neg. Participle	,, *de* or *zu*	not being.
Hypothetical	,, *ba*	should (he) be.
Neg. Adjective	Wanting	
Future............	*Mashō*	(he) will be.
Imperative	*Mase*	be!
Present Indicative..	*Masŭ* or *masuru*	(he) is.
Neg. Imperative ..	*Masŭ-na!*	do not be!
Neg. of Future	,, *mai*	(he) will not be.
Conditional Base ..	*Masure*	
Conditional	*Masure-ba*	if (he) is.
Concessive	,, *do*	though (he) is.

§ 46. THE STEM* OR INDEFINITE FORM. *Kashi, tabe.*

1. As will have been seen from the above tables, the stem is used as a base to which some of the terminations are added.

2. The stem is used to form compounds with nouns, adjectives, or other verbs.

Examples.

Kashiya.	'A house to let,' from *kashi*, stem of *kasu*, 'to lend,' and *ya*, 'a house.'
Kimono.	'Clothes,' from *ki*, stem of *kiru*, 'to clothe,' and *mono*, 'a thing.'
Migurushi.	'Ugly,' from *mi*, stem of *miru*, 'to see,' and *kurushi*, painful, 'distressing.'
Arigatai.	'It is difficult to be' (I am much obliged), from *ari*, stem of *aru*, 'to be' and *katai*, 'hard, 'difficult.'
Buchikorosu.	'To beat to death,' from *buchi*, stem of *butsu*, 'to beat,' and *korosu*, 'to kill.'
Shiageru.	'To finish,' from *shi*, stem of *suru* 'to do,' and *ageru*, 'to raise.'

Sora wa kumotte imasŭ The sky is clouded; it looks
sky   clouded   is   like rain.
kara, furi-sōna ambai desŭ.
because fall   state

---

* The form which in previous editions of this work was termed the Root is now called the Stem or Indefinite Form for reasons which have been very convincingly put by Mr. B. H. Chamberlain in a short paper read before the Asiatic Society of Japan, to which I am indebted for this improvement. It is possible, however, that such stems as *kashi* are after all really roots, the *i* not being a termination but merely a sound added in order to comply with the rule that in Japanese every syllable must end with a vowel.

THE VERB. 51

Yō   sumi-shidai ni.   As soon as my business is
business finish order in   finished.

Deki   shidai ni okurimashō.   I will send it as soon as it is
is made order will send   made.

Furi-sōna (for *furi-sō-naru*), *sumi-shidai* and *deki-shidai* in these sentences should be regarded as compounds.

3. The stem is often a noun.

Examples.

O   kamai nasaimasuna.   Please don't mind.
(hon.) care   do not

O   wakari   mo   You will probably not under-
(hon.)   understanding   stand, but—
arimasūmai ga. —
will not be but

Mō   o kayeri ni natta.   He has already gone away.
already return has become

Naka-naka o kiki-ire   He utterly refused to listen to
middle-middle listen-take-in   me.
ga nakatta.
was not

Kono shina mochi wa yoro-   This article wears well.
this article hold   is
shi.
good

Shimai ni   natta.   It is finished.
end   to has become

Mi ni ikimashīta.   I went to see.
see to   went

Kai ni kimashīta.   I have come to buy.
buy to come

Cha wo nomi nagara.   Whilst drinking tea.
tea   drink whilst

Negative tenses are formed by prefixing the stem followed by the particle *wa* or *mo* to the negative forms of the verbs *suru* or *itasu*, 'to do.' These forms are more emphatic than the corresponding simple tenses of the verb, and are in very common use. *Wa* in this position is commonly pronounced *ya*.

Examples.

Kono minato ni kakureta iwa ari wa (or *ya*) *shinai ka?* harbour hidden rock is do not?	Are there no hidden rocks in this harbour?
Machi wa (or *ya*) *shimasenŭ.* wait do not	I won't wait.
Daremo ori wa itashimasenŭ. any one remain does not	There is nobody here.
Kamai ya shinai. care don't	I don't care.
Mada ki ya shimasŭmai. yet come will not do	He can't have come yet.
Shini wa itashimasŭmai. die will not do	He will not die.

4. The Stem is the subject of a rule of Syntax which is very important in the written language, and is occasionally exemplified in the spoken language.

Rule. When two or more consecutive clauses of a sentence contain verbs in the same mood and tense, the last verb only takes the distinctive termination of the mood and tense, and all those which precede are put in the stem or indefinite form, so called because it has no mood or tense of its own. In the case of Negative Forms, the indefinite form is the participle in *zu*.

This rule is the counterpart for verbs of the rule given for Adjectives in Chap. VII.

Examples.

Mame wo makeba, mame ga haye, asa no tane wo makeba, asa ga dekiru. beans if sow beans grow hemp seed if sow hemp . becomes.	If you sow beans, beans grow, and if you sow hemp seed, hemp grows.

THE VERB. 53

| Watakŭshi no yōna bimbō- nin wa zeni no aru toki ni wa kai, nai toki wa, kawanai. | A poor man like me buys when he has money, and does not buy when he has none. |
| I sort of poor man cash is time buy not time do not buy | |

| Tōkiō no hō ye o ide da to iu hito mo ari, yappari uchi ni o ide da to mo iu. ヽトえアル | There are people who say that he is going to Tokio, and it is also said that he is going to stay at home. |
| side go say people are still home at also say | |

| Miredomo, miyezu; kikedo- mo kikoyenai. | Though they look, they cannot see; though they listen, they cannot hear. |
| though see can't see though hear cannot hear | |

The student should not attempt to imitate this construction, which is not very common in ordinary conversation. Instead of *haye, kai,* it is better to say *hayeru ga, kau ga.* For *ari, areba* is better, and for *miyezu, miyenai.*

§ 47. THE PAST PARTICIPLE. *Kashite, tabete.*

The termination *te* of the past participle is really the stem of an obsolete verb *tsuru* 'to finish.' This accounts for its being occasionally like other stems used as a noun, as in the phrase *shitte no tōri* 'as you are aware.' It also follows that such phrases as *matte oru,* 'he is waiting,' are really examples of the rule of syntax given in the preceding section, *matte* being the Indefinite Form.

The term Past Participle is not free from objection, as this is by no means the only use of this form. It must sometimes be rendered by the present participle, and it sometimes has no reference to time, but describes the manner of the action of the verb which follows.

Examples.

Doko ye itte kita? — Where has he been to?
where having gone has come

Motte kite age-mashū. — I will bring it for you.
having taken having come I will offer

Kami wo kitte moratta. — I got my hair cut.
hair having cut received

Dare ka Yokohama made itte moraitai. — I want somebody to go to Yokohama for me.
somebody as far as having gone I wish to receive

Sono hagaki wo yonde nan'to itta? — What did he say when he read that post-card?
that post-card having read what said

Mūma ni wa notte miro; hito ni wa sotte miro. — Try a horse by riding him; try a man by associating with him.
horse riding see man associating see

Yōji ga atte no tagiō. — A journey on business.
business being journey

Tatte mo suwatte mo, nedan wa onaji koto. — It is as cheap sitting as standing.
standing sitting price same thing

O furo ni itte mo yoroshiu gozarimasū ka? — May I go to the bath?
bath having gone good is ?

Haitte mo daiji nai. — It does not matter, even if you come (or go) in.
having entered great thing is not

Itte shimatta. — He has gone away.
having gone has finished

Kashi wo tabete shimatta. — He has eaten all the cakes.
cakes eating has finished

THE VERB. 55

Amari tabete wa biōki ni naru.
too much   ill   become
You will become ill if you eat too much.

The last example shows that the Past Participle with *wa* added may be used as equivalent to the Conditional Form in *eba*. *Te wa* is in the common Tokio dialect pronounced *cha*. *Te wa* has not always the force of the Conditional.

Example.

Nete wa imasenū.   He is not gone to bed.
having lain down remains not

Note the difference in meaning between *kashite kara*, 'after lending,' and *kashita kara*, 'because he lent.'

§ 48. THE PAST TENSE. *Kashita, tabeta.*

The *ta* of the past tense is a shortened form of *taru*, which is itself contracted for *te-aru*, *te* being the termination of the past participle, and *aru* the verb 'to be.'

In the written language *taru* has a perfect signification, the simple past tense being indicated by the particle *shi* or *ki* added to the stem. These latter forms are obsolete in the spoken language, where *ta* is oftener a simple past than a perfect, although the latter use is not unknown. *Yokohama ye itta* may mean, either 'he went to Yokohama,' or 'he has gone to Yokohama.' If it is desired to bring out the perfect signification distinctly, the past participle with *oru* or *iru* is employed, as *Yokohama ye itte oru*, *itte iru* or *itteru*, 'he has gone to Yokohama,' lit. 'having gone to Yokohama he remains.'

Like the other tenses of the Indicative Mood, the Past Tense may stand to other words in the relation (1), of a Verb, as *ano hito wa kita*, 'he came or has come,' (2), of an Adjective,* as *kita hito,* 'the came man' i.e. 'the man who has come,' or (3), of a Noun, as *kita ni sōi nai* 'there is no mistake about his having come.'

• Examples of the Past Tense.

1. As a Verb.

Kiō kita.	He came to-day.
to-day came	
Dō shimashita?	What has happened to him?
how has done	

The past tense is sometimes used where in English the present is preferred, as *wakarimashita* 'I understand.'

2. As an Adjective.

Kono aida kashita kane.	The money I lent some
this interval lent money	days ago.
Kesa tabemashita nashi.	The pears I ate this morning.
this morning. ate pear	
Kionen no fuyu watakūshi no	The man who came to my
last year winter my	place in the winter of last year.
tokoro ni kita hito.	
place came man	
Kane wo tameta uye de	He is going back to his
money collected upon	country after he has amassed
kuni ni kayeru.	some money.
country returns	

The past tense, as an adjective, is frequently followed by the particle *no.*

Examples.

Nita no yori wa yaketa no	I prefer roast to boiled.
boiled than roast	
yoroshiu gozarimasū.	
good is	
Shinda no ja nai ka?	Is it not a dead one?
dead is not?	
Ima jibun maitta no ga	Am I wrong to have come at
now time came	this time?
warui ka?	
is bad?	

---

* Cf. § 28 Relative Pronoun.

Shimbun	no	koto	de	It seems they have come
newspaper		thing		about the newspaper.
kimashita	sō	desū.		
come		it is		

3. As a Noun.

Itta	ga	yokatta.	I wish I had gone ('I am glad I
the having gone		was good	went' would be *itta no wa yokatta*).

Maketa	ni	chigai	There is no mistake about his
the being beaten		mistake	having been beaten.
wa nai.			
is not			

Tori-otoshita	wo mireba.	When I looked at what he
take dropped	when saw.	had dropped.

Hiroi-totte	kureta	What sort of a person was it
pick up having taken	gave	who picked it up for me?
wa dō	iu hito de atta?	
how	called man was	

Takke, a contraction for *tari-keru* of the written language, is sometimes employed as a sort of past termination. It is however used only as a verb, and not as an adjective or noun, and generally indicates that the speaker is in doubt or trying to remember.

Examples.

Ano otoko	wa	nan'	to	What *was* that man's name?
that man		what		
mōshimashitakke?				
called				

Ā! sayō deshitakke!	Ah! that is how it was!
ah! thus it was	

Chotto! nan' to ka iimashi-	I say! what is this your
a little what called	name is? Shall I say O Kane?
takke; moshi o Kane don ka?	
suppose ?	

Don shows that it is a servant who is addressed.

§ 49. THE CONDITIONAL AND THE HYPOTHETICAL FORMS OF THE PAST TENSE. *Kashitareba, tabetareba.*

Tareba, taraba are for *te areba, te araba*. *Tareba* is commonly still further contracted into *tara*.

There was originally a distinction between *tareba* and *taraba*, the former relating to an event which has actually happened or is probable, the use of the latter implying that the event has not happened at all, or is put as a mere supposition. But this distinction is now lost and both forms are used indiscriminately, there being a tendency for *taraba* to fall out of use.

Kashitareba may mean not only 'if he lent,' but 'if he* had lent,' 'if he shall have lent,' 'since he has lent,' 'when he lent,' 'when he had lent,' 'when he shall have lent.'

The compound tense *kashita nara* is very generally used in much the same sense as *kashitareba*. *Nara* is here for *nareba*, the Conditional Present of *naru*, 'to be.'

Examples of *tareba*, *taraba*, *tara* and *ta nara*.

Sore ga wakattareba, ato wa yasui. that when have understood rest is easy	If (or when) we have understood that, the rest is easy.
Tōkiō ye ikimashitareba chūmon shimashō. when I have gone to Tokio order will do	As soon as I have gone to Tokio, I will order some.
Sō mōshimashitareba, mina okorimashita. so when I said all flew into a passion	When I said so, they all flew into a passion.
Benten wo tootara kaji ga dekimashita. when passed fire was made	When I passed Benten, a fire broke out.
Ittaraba, kayō na koto wa dekinai hadzu de arimashita. if had gone this kind of thing not become necessity was	If he had gone, nothing of this kind could have happened.

---

* It may be well to repeat here a remark which has been already made, viz., that the Japanese Verb has no person, and that where the pronoun 'he' is introduced in the English version, any other pronoun would do as well.

THE VERB. 59

| Kitaraba taihen da. | It would be a terrible thing if |
| if should come great change is | he came. |

Shinimashitareba dō suru? What would you do, if he died?
if died how do

Oya ga shinimashitara dō   If his parents had died, what
parents   if died   how   would he have done?
shimashitarō?
would have done

Isshoni kitareba yok'atta.   It would have been well if he
together if had come good was   had come along with us.

O! dare ka to omottara,   Oh! I wondered who it was.
oh! who   while I thought   Mr. Fujita?
Fujita kun ka.
Mr. ?

Iwanŭ to mōshitara,   I thought he would not tell,
not say that when he said   when he had once said he
kanarazu inmai to   would not.
certainly will not say that
zonjimashita.
thought

Kowashita nara, naze kowa-   If you broke it, why not let
broke   if   why broke   me know that you broke it?
shita to watakŭshi ni, koto-
me   to explana-
wari wo iwanai ka?
tion   not say ?

§ 50. THE PROBABLE PAST, OR PERFECT FUTURE. *Ka-shitarō, tabetarō*.

The termination *tarō* of this tense is a contraction for *te arō*, *arō* being the future of *aru* 'to be.'

It is little used as a noun or adjective, although theoretically it might be so employed.

Examples.

Mō shimai ni narimashi-   It is probably (or will be)
already finish   will have   finished by this time.
tarō.
become

THE VERB.

Dō iu wake de gozari-
how called reason will have
mashitarō?
been

What could have been the reason?

Kimashitarō ka?
Do you think he has come?

Detarō.
He has probably gone out.

Sazo go taikutsŭ de gozari-
surely ennui will have
mashitaro.
been

You must surely have found the time long.

§ 51. THE ALTERNATIVE FORM. *Kashitari, tabetari.*

The termination *tari* of this form is a contraction for *te ari.*

A Verb in this form is nearly always accompanied by one or more other verbs in the same form.

Examples.

Oya ni kokorodzŭkai kake-
parents anxiety hung
tari, oya wo nakasetari no fu-
make weep un-
kō wo aratameta.
filial conduct reformed

He reformed his unfilial conduct in now giving anxiety to his parents, and now making them weep.

Kono ame ga futtari yandari
this rain falling stopping
suru tenki wa ki ni iranai.
do weather mind not enter

I don't like this weather, when it is alternately raining and leaving off.

Tenugui ni tsutsundari tamoto
towel wrapping up sleeve
ye iretari shite.
putting in doing

Wrapping up some in his towel and putting others into his sleeve.

Jitsu ni negattari kanattari
truly begging granting
de gozarimasŭ.
is

Indeed it is a case of no sooner asked for than granted.

Anata wa hito wo koroshita-
you people killing
ri zoku wo hataraku kokoro wa
robbery work heart
arimasenŭ to.
is not if

If you have no wish to commit murder or robbery.

Midzu wo kundari nani ka   Please draw water for me,
water   drawing something   and the like.
shite o kure.
doing   give

The termination *tari* originally had no alternative meaning, and in some of the above phrases the alternative force is not very evident.

§ 52. THE CONCESSIVE PAST. *Kashitaredo, tabetaredo.*

This form is not much used, being replaced by *kashita to iyedo*, lit. 'though one say that (he) lent,' or more commonly still, by *kashita keredo. Mo* 'even' is often added to all these forms. 'Though' is the correct translation of the concessive terminations but it is usually more convenient to render them in English by placing 'but' at the beginning of the subsequent clause.

Example.

Yohodo maye ni kane wo   I lent him money a long
much before money   time ago, but he has not
kashita keredo, mada kayeshi-   returned it yet.
lent although yet returned
masenu.
not

Kashite mo is also much used with nearly the same meaning, but it is of no special tense, and may be either present, past or future.

§ 53. DESIDERATIVE ADJECTIVE. *Kashitai, tabetai.* See Chap. VII.

§ 54. THE POLITE FORM. *Kashimasu, tabemasu.* The conjugation of this form is given in § 45. For its use, see Chap. XII.

§ 55. THE NEGATIVE BASE. *Kasa, tabe* are not in use as separate words. This form has no meaning by itself.

§ 56. THE NEGATIVE PRESENT INDICATIVE. *Kasanŭ, tabenŭ.*

The final *u* of this form is inaudible, except when very distinct pronunciation is aimed at. The Japanese themselves often omit it in writing the spoken language.

Instead of this form, the Tokio dialect generally prefers the Negative Adjective *kasanai, tabenai.* (See Chap. VII.)

Like the other tenses of the Indicative Mood, the Negative Present may be either a verb, an adjective or a noun. (See remarks on the Past Tense.)

Examples.

1. As a Verb.

Kane ga dekinŭ to, hō-   If money is not procured,
money is not made if all   there will be duns coming from
bō kara kakctori ga kuru d'arō.   all quarters.
sides from dun   come will

Shiranŭ.   I don't know.

Arc kiri (pron. *arckkiri*)   I have never seen him since.
that cut off
aimasenŭ.
not meet

(The last example shows that this form is sometimes used where we have a past tense.)

Sora! warawanŭ to mōshi-   There! have you not laughed
that! not laugh   having   after having said you would not?
te, waratta de wa nai ka?
said laughed (pred.) is not?

(This example illustrates the principle that in Japanese there are no special forms for indirect narration. If a man says *warawanŭ* 'I won't laugh' the same word *warawanŭ* is used in repeating what he said, though in English we change 'will' into 'would.' For *warawanŭ* as a future see the section on the Future Form).

2. As an Adjective.

Shiranŭ koto wa gozarima-   He certainly knows.
not-know thing   is
senŭ.
not

Shiranŭ koto aru mono   Don't tell me you don't know.
not-know thing existing thing
ka? (vulgarly *monka*).
is?

THE VERB. 63

Dekinŭ toki wa shikata ga nai. not-can-do time do-manner is not	If it can't be done, there is no help for it.
Shiranŭ hito.	A man whom I don't know. (also, a man who does not know.)
Yeigo wakaranŭ hito. English words not-understand man	A man who does not understand English.
Ichi nen mo tatanŭ uchi ni. one year even not-stand within	Before even a year had passed.

3. As a Noun.

Shirimasenŭ de gozaimasŭ. not-know is	I don't know (a very humble form of expression used by people of the lower classes to their superiors).
Dōmo shi ya shi nai kara nigenŭ de mo ii. any how do do not because the not-running-away even is good.	You needn't run away, I won't do anything to you.
O ki ni iranŭ wo o naoshi nasare. (hon.) mind not-enter mend do	Correct what displeases you (in me).

A number of Compound Tenses are formed by adding *de arō, de atta*, etc., to the Negative Form (or the Neg. Adj.) taken as a noun.

Examples.

Shiranŭ d'arō. not-knowing will be	He probably does not know.
Kamawanŭ d'attarō. not-caring probably was	He probably did not care.

§ 57. THE NEGATIVE PAST. *Kasananda, tabenanda.* This form is usually replaced in the Tokio dialect by *kasanakatta, tabenakatta*, the predicate form of the negative adjectives (*kasanaku tabenaku*) combined with the past tense of *aru*, 'to be,' the *u* final being elided before the *a* of *aru*.

Kasanŭ (or *kasanai*) *de atta* may also be used to express the same meaning.

Examples.

Ikimasenanda.	I did not go.
Sonnani yasuku wa urananda so cheap did-not-sell (or *uranakatta*).	I did not sell it so cheap as that.
Hanashi ni ukarete ki ga talk on floated mind *tsukananda.* not-stick	I was so taken up by the conversation that I did not notice it.

A Japanese often uses the negative of the present tense or the negative adjective where the past seems to us more suitable. Thus, in answer to the question, Did you go? *O ide nasatta ka?* the reply will very likely be, *Ikimasenŭ*, for 'I did not go.'

This is particularly true in the case of indirect clauses or where the Negative Past, if used, would be an adjective or a noun.

Examples.

Chūmon shīta ka senŭ ka to order did ? do not ? *iu koto wo hanashite* called thing talking *otta.* remained	They were discussing the question of whether it had been ordered or not. (Note that the Japanese prefers the Active to the Passive construction).
Kiō made itoma wo negawa- to-day until leave not- *nai mono.* request person	Those who have not resigned up till to-day.

From the Negative Past are formed a Negative Past Alternative, *kasanandari, tabenandari,* a Negative Past Conditional, *kasanandareba, tabenandareba,* a Negative

Past Hypothetical, *kasanandaraba, tabenandaraba*, a Negative Past Concessive, *kasanandaredo, tabenandaredo*, and a Negative Probable Past, *kasanandarō, tabenandarō*. These forms have not been included in the scheme of conjugation, as most of them are not very common, and their formation is very simple. Like other negative forms they are frequently replaced by compound tenses formed with the help of the Negative Adjective.

§ 58. THE NEGATIVE CONDITIONAL. *Kasaneba, tabeneba.*

These are the negative forms corresponding to the positive forms *kaseba, tabereba.*

Example.

| *Miōnichi made tsŭkuraneba,* to-morrow until if not make *hoka de atsurayeru.* elsewhere order | If he does not make it by to-morrow I shall order it somewhere else. |

This part of the verb followed by the negative of *naru*, 'to become,' gives the force of the English auxiliary verb 'must,' as in the following example:—

| *Mawaraneba naranŭ.* if not go round does not become | I must go round. |
| *Te wo arawaneba naranŭ.* hand if not wash | I must wash my hands. |

The *naranŭ* is sometimes allowed to be understood, as in the following example:—

| *Ikaneba.* | I must go. |

The Negative Adjective followed by *te wa* is used in the same way, and is commoner. See Chap. VII.

The final *ba* of the Negative Conditional is often pronounced *ya*.

For 'if he does not lend' one can also say *kasanakereba, kasanŭ kereba, kasanŭ toki wa, kasanai toki wa, kasanŭ* *nara, kasanai nara, kasanŭ to, kasanai to, kasanaku te wa* or *kasanai de wa,* though some slight distinctions might be drawn in the meaning and application of these phrases.*

§ 59. THE NEGATIVE HYPOTHETICAL. *Kasazuba, tabezuba.*

Kasazuba, tabezuba are the negatives corresponding to *kasaba, tabeba.* They have sometimes an *m* inserted for euphony before the termination *ba.* In practice they are confounded with the conditional forms.

Examples.

Konnichi ame ga furazuba, to-day rain if not fall *Tsukiji ye o tomo accompanying itashitō gozaimasŭ.* wish-to-do am	I want to go with you to Tsukiji, if it does not rain today.
Shōshō kinsu wo tsukawasazuba narimasŭmai. a little money if not spend will not become	It will be necessary to spend a little money.

§ 60. THE NEGATIVE CONCESSIVE. *Kasanedo, tabenedo.*

Example.

Hakodate ye itte minedo, going see not *yohodo samui yŭsu de* very cold seem *gozaimasŭ.* is	Though I have not gone to Hakodate and seen for myself, I am informed that it is very cold there.

This form is not much used, being ordinarily replaced by the Negative Present or Negative Adjective followed by *keredo.* For *kasanedo,* one nearly always hears *kasanŭ keredo* or *kasanai keredo.*

§ 61. THE NEGATIVE PARTICIPLES. *Kasade, kasazu, tabede, tabezu.*

THE VERB. 67

De as a negative termination is commoner in the western dialects than in the Tokio language.

The Negative Participle has, like the past participle, the syntax of the Stem or Indefinite Form.

As a Stem it is usually a noun.

Examples.

Negai wo togezu ni shinda.
wish   not obtaining died
He died without obtaining his wish.

Mŭma ni kaiba wo tsŭkezu ni itte shimatta.
horse   fodder giving not having gone finished
He went away without giving the horse his food.

Hambun kikazu ni demashita.
half   not hearing went out
He went out without hearing half.

Kare kore iwazu ni totte koi.
that this not saying   having taken come
Don't make objections, but bring it here.

Mizu,   shirazu   no mono.
not seeing not knowing person
A person one has never seen or heard of.

Mukō mizu wo suru hito de wa nai.
opposite not seeing   man   is not
He is not a man who does reckless things.

Ikazu ni shimaimashita.
without going he finished
He never went after all.

In the following sentence this form has an adverbial force.

Ai-kawarazu tassha de gozaimasŭ.
unchangingly robust   is
He is in his usual robust health.

In the following examples it is a verb.

Shōyŭ wa irezu to yoroshiŭ gozaimasŭ.
sauce not put in if good   is
You need not put in any sauce (soy).

Sonna koto wo iwazu to, Don't talk like that, but give
such thing not saying him the money.
kane wo yare.
money give

Kasazŭ de, kasanai de are much used as substitutes for *kasazu.*

As stated above (§ 47), the Neg. Participle in *zu* may have the force of the Indefinite Form.

Example.

Hajime wa goku shimbiō At first he was an excellent
beginning very admirable servant, but he gradually got
d'atta ga; oi oi zōchō stuck up and would not pay the
was gradually increasing slightest attention to my orders,
shite, iitsŭkeru koto wa sŭkoshi and in addition he is constantly
doing order thing a little trying to deceive me by telling
mo kikazu, sono uye lies.
even not hear that over and
 (*Kikazu* here takes its tense from *da* at
uso wo tsuite oira wo the end of the sentence and is therefore
above falsehood telling me to be translated as if it were *kikanŭ*,
azamuku koto tabi tabi da. the Neg. Present Indicative.)
deceive thing frequently is.

§ 62. HYPOTHETICAL FORM. *Kasaba, tateba:*
This form is gradually falling out of use. It ought to imply a hypothesis or bare supposition, but in speaking it is mostly confounded with the Conditional Form in *ba.*

There are however some locutions where it is still preferred to the Conditional.

Example.

Ano hĭto wa iwaba He is, so to speak, an upper
that man if one say class society buffoon.
jōtō shakai no taiko-mochi
first class society buffoon
de gozaimasŭ.

Other examples of the Hypothetical Form.

Ichido naraba, medzurashiku If it were once, there would be
one time if it were curious nothing extraordinary about it.
mo nai.
even is not.

Teppō	*motaba,*	*uchi-korosu*	If I had a gun, I would shoot him.
gun	if had	hit kill	
no desū.			
is			

O rusu	*naraba kono tegami wo*		If he is not at home, bring back this letter.
absent	if is this letter		
motte	*kayere.*		
taking	come back.		

The termination *ba* of this form is identical with the particle *wa* described in Chapter IX, but it is doubtful whether *kasaba* may not stand for *kasan* (the old future) *wa* or perhaps *kasan ni wa*. It will be remembered that *ba* is *wa* with the *nigori*. See §. 4.

§ 63. THE NEGATIVE ADJECTIVE. *Kasanai, tabenai.*

This form is conjugated as an Adjective. It is much used in various combinations as a substitute for the negative forms of the verb. See Chap. VII.

§ 64. THE FUTURE. *Kasō, tabeyō.*

The formation of the Future presents some difficulty. The written language forms the future of all verbs by adding *n* (originally *mu**) to the negative base, thus, *kasan, taben, dekin*. In the spoken language this *n* becomes *u*, which in the first conjugation is contracted with the preceding *a* into *ō*, thus giving the form *kasō*. In the same way *taben* and *dekin* ought to become *tabyō* (*e* being considered equal to *i+a*), *dekiu*, and these forms are actually in use in some dialects, but the Tokio language, by a mistaken analogy, has adopted the forms *tabeyō, dekiyō*.

The following practical rule for forming the future may be found useful.

Rule.—For the first conjugation change *u* of the Present Indicative into *ō*. For the second conjugation add *yō* to the stem.

---

* It may be conjectured that *mu* contains the same root as *miru*, 'to see,' and that the original meaning of *kasa-mu* or *kasan* was "lend-seem."

It is convenient to call *kasō* the Future and *kasu* the Present, but in practice the distinction between these forms is less often one of time than that *kasō* expresses an opinion or a probability (as 'will' sometimes does in English) and *kasu* a fact. *Kasō* may be translated 'he probably lends,' 'I think he lends,' or 'he probably will lend'; *kasu* is a positive assertion, and may be rendered according to circumstances 'he lends,' or 'he will lend.' If a Japanese says *miōnichi mairimashō*, it must not be thought that he is promising faithfully to come to-morrow. He has only said 'I shall most probably come to-morrow.' If he intends to give a definite promise, he will say, *miōnichi mairimasŭ*.

These remarks also apply to the Negative Future and Present, *kasumai*, *kasanŭ*.

Examples of the Future.

1. As a Noun. This tense is not much used as a noun.

Itte miyō ja nai ka?	
having gone shall see is not ?	Shall we not go and see it?

2. As an Adjective, *kasō* does not often occur, the Present Indicative being used instead. Thus for 'the ship which will arrive the day after to-morrow' we say *asatte chaku suru* (not *shō*) *fune*. There are however certain phrases where the future is used before nouns.

Narō koto naraba.	If it can be done.
will become thing if it is	
Shiyō koto ga nai.	There is nothing which can be done.
will do thing is not	
Shirō hadzu wa nai.	He can't possibly know.
will know necessity is not	

3. As a Verb.

Nan'd' arō?	What can it be?
what will be	

Go de mo hajimeyō ka?	Shall we begin a game of *go*?
Koyō mo shirenū. will come even can't know	He may come for aught I know.
Sono hinkō wa tadashī- That conduct correct *karō ga—* will be but—	His conduct may very likely be correct but—
Yūbin haitatsŭ nin wo post distribution man *utō to shīta.* strike (fut.) did	He made to strike the postman.
Konrei no sakadzuki wo shō wedding wine cup do *to in tokoro.* called place	Just when they were about to exchange the marriage wine-cup.
Nagasaki ni honya aru ka? book shop	Are there any bookshops in Nagasaki?
Arimashō.	I believe there are.
Gozarimasŭmai.	I am afraid not.
Hatoba ni kayoi-bune ga arō jetty ferry boat *ka?*	Do you think there are any ferry boats at the jetty?
Arimasŭ to mo.	To be sure there are.
Miōnichi sono mŭma wo to-morrow horse *kaimashō.* will buy	I shall probably buy that horse to-morrow.
Itsu shuppan shimashō ka? when sailing will do	When is she likely to sail?
Miōnichi jiu ni ji ni shuppan to-morrow *suru.*	She sails at twelve o'clock to-morrow.

§ 65. THE PRESENT INDICATIVE. *Kasu, taberu.*

The Form which is now used as a Present Indicative had formerly in the case of verbs of the Second Conjugation the force of an Adjective or Noun only, a different form being in use for the Indicative Mood. *Taberu* (or *taburu*, as it was then pronounced, and still is pronounced in the central and western provinces) could only be used before a noun, as *taburu hito*, 'the man who eats,' or as a noun itself in the sense of 'eating.' It could not mean 'he eats,' to express which there was a distinct form viz. *tabu*. In the modern spoken language *tabu* has fallen out of use and *taburu* (altered to *taberu* in Tokio) alone is employed for the Indicative Mood as well as in its other capacities as an Adjective or Noun. I suspect that this change had its origin in the habit which the Japanese are prone to of leaving their sentences unfinished. They perhaps began a sentence by saying *kono hito ga taberu wa*—'this man's eating '—intending to add words indicating that his eating is a fact, but leaving them ultimately unsaid. This becoming a general practice, *kono hito ga taberu wa* or *kono hito ga taberu* came to mean 'this man eats.' This explanation is confirmed by the fact that even in the modern colloquial we find such sentences as *kono hito ga taberu wa* (or *wa e, e* being a slightly emphatic particle) where the meaning is simply 'this man eats.' It is difficult to see what business the *wa* has here, if something has not been omitted.

In the First Conjugation, the Present Indicative and its Adjective Form have always been identical, so that no change is apparent, but in the Irregular Verbs *aru* and *naru*, the Indicatives of which were originally *ari* and *nari*, and in Adjectives, a similar alteration has taken place.

An interesting consequence of this change is that *ga*, which in the older language was a possessive particle only, has in the modern colloquial become the sign of the nominative case. If *taberu* in the sentence *kono hito ga taberu* no longer means 'eating' but 'eats,' it follows of necessity that *ga* must also change its signification and that *kono hito ga* will mean not 'this man's,' but 'this man.'

Examples of the Present Indicative.

1. As a Noun.

Damatte oru ga i. silent remaining is good	You had better hold your tongue.
Iku ni chigai nai. going mistake is not	There is no mistake about his going.
Iku yori wa ikanai going than not going *hō ga yoroshi.* side is good	It is better not to go than to go.
Shinjiru to shinjinai to believing not believing *wa hito no jiyū desŭ.* man liberty is	A man is at liberty to believe or not to believe.
Sō suru ni. doing	In doing so.

THE VERB.

Sore wo miru ni.   In looking at it.
that   seeing

Remember that *ni* after the stem means 'in order to' as—

Nani shi ni kita?   What have you come to do?
what do to have come

Kasa wo kari ni   I have come to borrow an
umbrella borrow   umbrella.
mairimashĭta.
have come

2. As an Adjective.

Sankei suru hĭto   The people who come to wor-
come-worship do man   ship are many.
ga ōi.
are many

Taberu mono ga nai.   I have got nothing to eat.
eat thing is not

Sō suru hi ni wa.   On the day you do that. If you
so do day on   do that.

Motoyori hiki-oi ga hara-   It is a matter of course when a
of course liabilities not   man can't pay his debts that he
warenai toki wa tsubureru no   should smash up.
can pay time smash up
wa mochiron no koto desŭ.
of course thing is

Miōnichi yo-ake ni shut-   You must make everything
to-morrow day break at start-   quite ready so as to start at day-
tatsŭ suru yōni chanto   break tomorrow.
ing do manner in perfectly
shĭtaku wo shinakŭ cha
preparation if not make
ikenai.
does not do

3. As a Verb.

Dare ka soto de matsŭ.   Somebody is waiting outside.
somebody outside waits

Ka ga taisō oru.   There are a great many mus-
musquito many abide   quitoes.

Konnichi nara (for *nareba*),   If today, it is in time.
to-day
ma ni au.
space meets

Yō ga areba, te wo tataku.
business if is hands strike

If I have anything for you to do, I will clap my hands. (Observe that the present is used here, not the future, there being no doubt.)

Jiu ri nara, kuwazu ni
ten if it were not eating
de mo iku ga, hiaku ri desŭ
even could (or 100 is
 would) go
kara—
because

If it were ten *ri*, I could (or would) go even without· eating, but as it is 100 *ri*—

Konnichi o taku ye agaru
to-day (hon.) house to go up
no desŭ ga, ashi ga itamimashi-
 is leg being pain-
te, (ikaremasŭmai).
ful (shall not be able to go)

I would go to your house to-day, but as I have a bad leg,— (I am afraid I shall not be able to go).

§ 66. THE NEGATIVE IMPERATIVE. *Kasuna, taberuna.*

Examples.

Ikuna ! — Don't go!
Shōchi suruna ! — Don't consent!
Sore wo taberuna ! — Don't eat that.

§ 67. THE NEGATIVE FUTURE. *Kasumai, tabemai.*

The termination *mai* of this tense is attached to the Present Indicative in the First, and to the Negative Base in the Second conjugation.

The Negative Adjective followed by *arō*, future of *aru*, 'to be,' is sometimes used for this form as, *shiranak'arō*, 'he probably does not know,' for *shiranai*. *Shiranŭ darō, shiranai darō* have also the same meaning.

For the true meaning of the Future see §. 64.

Examples of Negative Future.

Miōnichi made naorima-
tomorrow till recover
sŭmai.
will not

He won't be better by tomorrow.

Hïtori de dekimai. alone will not be able	Alone he will not be able.
Arumai.	I don't think there are any.
Meshi wo tabemai. rice will not eat	He is not likely to eat rice.
Ashïta ni mo naorumai mono de mo nai. tomorrow not recover thing even is not	It is possible he may recover even tomorrow.

§ 68. THE IMPERATIVE MOOD. *Kase, tabero.*

The Conditional Base is not in use as a separate word, except in the First Conjugation, where it coincides with the Imperative. In the Second Conjugation *ro*, or in the western dialect *yo*, is added to the root in order to form the Imperative.

Instead of the bare Imperative, which is a very rough style of address, it is generally preferable to use some of the minor honorifics, even when addressing servants. Instead of *to wo shimero*, it is better to say *to wo shimete, to wo shimete o kure* or *to wo shime na* (for *shime nasare*).

Examples.

Achi ike! there go	Get away!
To wo shimero! door shut	Shut the door!
Kono hako wo akero! this box open	Empty this box. Open this box.
Waki ye yore! side approach	Go to one side!
Shïta ni iro! down remain	Squat down (as was formerly done by Japanese when a man of rank was passing).
Ten no bachi da to akiramero. heaven punishment is make up your mind	Make up your mind that it is a punishment from heaven.

Nani ni shiro, warui koto da. what make bad thing it is	Anyhow it is a bad business.
Shikkari shiro. firmly do	Bear up! (to a sick person) steady!
Osok'are hayak'are kōin ni narimashō. be it late be it early arrest will become	He will be arrested sooner or later.

§ 69. THE CONDITIONAL FORM. *Kaseba, tabereba.* Properly speaking there is the same distinction between this form and the Hypothetical Form *kaseba, tabeba*, that there is between the forms in *tareba* and *taraba*, i.e., the former denotes a condition either realized, or looked upon as likely to be so, while the forms in *aba* represent a mere hypothesis. But this distinction is almost wholly neglected in practice, and the forms in *eba* and *aba* are used indiscriminately. All the hypothetical forms, however, seem to be gradually falling out of use and are not much employed except in particular phrases. A distinction between these forms is always observed by correct writers.

Nareba, the conditional of *naru* 'to be', is nearly always contracted into *nara*.

Examples of Conditional Forms.

Asŭko ye ikeba, isshō komaru koto nashi. there to if go one life trouble thing is not	If I go there, I shall have no annoyance all my life.
Warui koto sureba, warui mukui ga aru. bad thing if do bad reward is	If you do evil, there is an evil reward.
Mōseba kayette kurō wo kakeyō to omotta. if tell on the contrary (hon.) anxiety hang thought	I thought that if I were to tell you, I should on the contrary cause you anxiety.

THE VERB. 77

Areba ii to omotte.
if there are is good thinking

Hoping (not a confident hope) there might be some.

Dorobō to ka nan' to ka iyeba yoi no ni.
thief ? something ? if say is good while

While he would have been justified in calling him a thief, or the like.

§ 70. THE CONCESSIVE FORM. *Kasedo, tabedo.*

This Form is mostly superseded by the Present Indicative followed by *keredo* or, more rarely, by *to iyedo*. Both these expressions may be used with any tense of the Indicative Mood, thus producing a series of Concessive Tenses. They may also be added to adjectives. *Keredo* is the Concessive Form of *keru*, which is probably the perfect tense of *kuru'* 'to come,' and *iyedo*, the Concessive Form of *iu*, 'to say,, so that *to iyedo* means literally 'though one say that.'

Mo, 'even,' is frequently added to all the Concessive Forms.

Examples.

Tenki naredo samui.
weather though it is is cold

Though fine, it is cold.

Kusuri wo nomedo naoranai.
medicine though drink not recovers

He will not recover, even though he do (or does) take medicine.

Tōnin wa sayō mōshita de mo arimashō keredomo, sore wa dōmo chito shinjiraremasenŭ.
person in question thus said even will be although that somehow a little cannot believe

The man himself may very likely have said so, but I can hardly believe it.

Tadzunemashita keredomo, gozaimasenŭ.
inquired although is not

I inquired, but there was none.

Kite iru to iyedomo.
having come remains though

Although he has come.

In speaking Japanese, the student should not use the Concessive Form standing by itself or the Form with *to iyedo*. They occur so seldom that Mr. Satow's *Kwaiwa Hen*, I believe, does not contain a single example of them. The Indicative Mood (or Attributive form of Adjectives) followed by *keredo* or *keredomo* is better, or he may use the past participle followed by *mo* (*kashitemo*), or the adverbial form of the adjective followed by *temo* (*osoku temo*).

DERIVATIVE VERBS.

§ 71. Transitive and Intransitive Verbs.

In English, there are seldom distinct words or forms for the transitive and intransitive applications of the same verbal root. Thus the words *ride*, *sink*, *break*, *bend* and many others are either transitive or intransitive according to circumstances. In such cases, the Japanese language has usually two distinct verbs containing the same root.

No rule can be given for forming transitive or intransitive verbs, but some of the more common modes of doing so are exemplified below :—

Intransitive.	Transitive.
Tatsu (1st. Conj.), to stand.	*Tateru* (2nd. Conj.), to set up.
Susumu (1st. (Conj.), to advance.	*Susumeru* (2nd. Conj.), to encourage.
Yamu (1st. Conj.), to cease.	*Yameru* (2nd. Conj.), to cease.
Iru (1st Conj.), to enter.	*Ireru* (2nd. Conj.), to put in.
Sagaru (1st Conj.), to come down.	*Sageru* (2nd. Conj.), to let down.

THE VERB. 79

Waku (1st. Conj.), to boil.
Wakasu (1st Conj.), to make boil.

Chiru (1st Conj.), to scatter.
Chirasu (1st. Conj.), to scatter.

Neru (2nd. Conj.), to sleep.
Nekasu (1st. Conj.), to put to sleep.

Oriru (2nd. Conj.), to descend.
Orosu (1st. Conj.), to lower.

Deru (2nd. Conj.), to go out.
Dasu (1st. Conj.), to put out.

The Intransitive Verbs illustrated in the following examples form a separate class. They have usually a potential force, but must not be confounded with the passive forms of the same verbs.

Kireru (2nd. Conj.), to be discontinuous.
Kiru (1st. Conj.), to cut.

Ureru (2nd. Conj.), to be saleable, to sell.
Uru (1st. Conj.), to sell.

Miyeru (2nd. Conj.), to be visible, to be able to see.
Miru (2nd Conj.), to see.

Kikoyeru (2nd. Conj.), to be audible, to be able to hear.
Kiku (1st. Conj.), to hear.

Ikeru (2nd. Conj.), to be able to go.
Iku (1st Conj.), to go.

The French *se couper*, *se vendre* correspond pretty accurately to *kireru*, *ureru*. The example *ikeru* shows that these verbs may be formed from intransitive as well as from transitive verbs. *Ikeru* is familiar to us in the negative adjective form *ikenai*, 'it is no go', 'it won't do'.

Note that while the termination *eru* may belong either to the transitive or to the intransitive form, verbs ending in *su* are transitive only. Exception. *Dasu* in combination is sometimes intransitive, as, *ame ga furi-dashīta*, 'it has come on to rain', *tobi-dashīta*, 'he rushed out'.

In the examples given below, we have pairs of transitive verbs containing the same root.

Karu (1st. Conj.), to borrow.   *Kasu* (1st. Conj.), to lend.

Adzukaru (1st. Conj.), to take charge of.   *Adzukeru* (2nd. Conj.) to give in charge.

Kiru (2nd. Conj.), to wear.   *Kiseru* (2nd. Conj.), to clothe.

Miru (2nd. Conj.), to see.   *Miseru* (2nd. Conj.), to show.

Examples of Transitive and Intransitive Verbs.

Yu   ga waita ka?
hot water   boiled?

Is the hot water ready?

He, ima wakashimasŭ de
yes now   make boil
gozaimasŭ.
it is

Yes, I am just getting it to boil.

Hara ga tatta.
belly arose

He got angry.

Umi-tate no tamago.
lay set up   egg

A new-laid egg.

Tatenai.
cannot stand

I cannot stand. I do not set up.

Bŏchan   wo nekashīte
(see Ch. XII.)   having put
kara, omaye mo nete
to bed after you   too having
        mo yoroshi.
gone to bed even is good

When you have put young master to bed, you can go too.

Betsŭdan   hima ga toreru
   particularly time   can take
hodo   no koto mo arimasŭmai.
amount   thing will not be

There probably won't be anything which will occupy any great time.

THE VERB. 81

Seken ye	*shirenai*	Before it becomes known to
world to	not become known	the world.
uchi ni.		
within		

Koko ja hanasenai		*yo.*	We can't talk here.
here	cannot talk	(emph. part.)	

Hitori	*mo*	*hanaseru*	There is not a single fellow
one man	even	can talk	worth talking to.
* *yatsu*	*wa*	*nai.*	
fellow		is not	

Taisō	*ni o*	*kawari*	How very much changed you
very much	(hon.)	change	are! enough to be unrecognizable
nasatta ne!	*Dashi-nuke ni*		if one met you all of a sudden.
done	abruptly		
attara,	*mi-chigayeru*	*gurai*	
if met	see can mistake	amount	
da.			
it is			

§ 72. CAUSATIVE VERBS.

Causative verbs are formed by adding *seru* to the Negative Base of verbs of the first conjugation, as *tsukuru* 'to make', *tsukuraseru* 'to cause to make.' In verbs of the second conjugation *saseru* is added to the stem, as *taberu* 'to eat,' *tabesaseru* 'to cause to eat.'

The causatives of the irregular verbs *kuru* and *suru* are *kosaseru* and *saseru*.

All causative verbs belong to the second conjugation.

Instead of the causative verbs, such phrases as *iku yō ni suru*, 'go-manner-make' i.e. 'to make him to go,' are much used.

The transitive verbs in *su* (1st. conj.) and the causatives in *seru* are constantly confounded, the same person saying for example at one time *kikashite* and at another *kikasete*.

Examples of Causative Verbs.

Taihen ni o dreadfully (honorific) *matase mōshita.* made to wait (respectful)	I have kept you waiting an awful time.
Mūma ni mame wo kuwaseta horse beans made eat *ka?*	Did you give the horse his beans?
Mo ichido kikasete more once having made hear *kudasare.* give	Please let me hear once more.
Kono ko ni kega wo sasete this child wound cause *sumanai.* not finish	It won't do to cause any hurt to this child.
Jiu ni shichi hachi wa ten seven eight *shōchi itasaseru kokoro de* agreement cause heart *gozarimasŭ.* is	I have an idea that it is seven or eight chances out of ten that I shall make him consent.
Fusoku nara, motto insufficient if is more *toraseyō.* will make take	If it is not enough, I will give you more.
Hontō no okka san ni reality mother *awasete kudasatta.* having made meet he gave	He was kind enough to cause her to meet her real mother.
A. *Musume ni muko wo* daughter to husband *torasete raku wo* having made take ease *shō to iu wake de wa* will make called reason *nai.* B. *Watakŭshi wa dō* is not I how *shite mo* having done even *torasenai.* do not make take	A. My reason for giving my daughter a husband is not that I intend to enjoy my ease. B. I will not allow her to take (a husband) on any account.

THE VERB. 83

§ 73. PASSIVE OR POTENTIAL VERBS.—Passive or Potential Verbs are formed by adding *areru* to the present indicative form of the active verbs, the final *u* of which is elided. Thus :—

Mirareru, to be seen, is formed from *miru*, to see.
Korosareru, to be killed,   ,,   ,, *korosu*, to kill.
Tadzunerareru, to be sought,   ,,   *tadzuneru*, to seek.

The passive forms of the irregular verbs *suru*, *kuru* are *serareru*, *korareru*.

The Passive verbs have also a Potential meaning. In the case of Intransitive verbs, this is their ordinary signification, although in such sentences as *teishi ni shinaremashita* 'she was died by her husband,' i.e. 'she was separated by death from her husband,' we have something like the passive of an intransitive verb.

The Passive Voice is much less used in Japanese than in English.

All passive verbs are of the 2nd. conjugation. 'By,' after a passive verb, is rendered in Japanese by *ni*.

Examples.

Jimmin ni kirawareru. people is hated	He is hated by his subjects.
Sendō ni tasŭkeraremashita. boatman was saved	He was saved by a boatman.
Miraremashita ka?	Could you see?
Ikareru de arō ka?	Will he be able to go?
Mairaremasenŭ.	I cannot come.
Kogoto iwaremashita. scolding he was said	He got a scolding.
Tanji no korosareru no wo being killed *mite.* having seen	On witnessing Tanji's murder.

Hachijiu	*yen to*	*iu*	He had taken from him the large sum of eighty *yen*.
eighty		called	
taikin	*wo*	*torareta.*	
large money		was taken	

Kane	*wo*	*torareyō*	I was nearly losing my money.
money		about to be taken	
to shita.			
made			

Omaye	*no o*	*kage*	*de*	Thanks to you I was not robbed of my money.
you		shadow	by	
kinsu	*wo*	*torarenai.*		
money		not taken		

Moraware ya itashi-masenŭ. — I can't accept it.
can accept   do not

Jissai bakari no otoko no — Led by the hand by a boy of about ten years old.
ten year amount   male
ko ni te wo hikarete.
child hand   being led

Shōhei no tame ni kawa no — He was kicked down by Shōhei into a deep part of the river. (*No tame ni* 'on account of' is also used for 'by' with the passive voice, but it is stiffer and less common).
          by   river
fukai tokoro ni ke-
deep place   kick
otosareta.
knocked down

A. *Sukkari gakumon wo* — A. I bid adieu to learning completely.
   wholly   learning
mi-kagitte   shimatta.
see-having limited finished

B. *Hate! umaku* — B. Well to be sure! that is a good one. I think it was a case of learning having bid adieu to you.
   well!   sweetly
itteru   ze;
say remain (emph. part.)
gakumon ni mi-kagirareta no
learning by see-limited
d'arō.
will be

Inu ni te wo kamareta. — He got his hand bitten by a dog. He was bitten on the hand by a dog.
dog   hand   was bitten

THE VERB. 85

In the terminations of Transitive, Intransitive, Causative and Passive Verbs, it is easy to distinguish the verbs *suru* 'to do,' *aru* 'to be' and *eru* 'to get.' The termination *areru* of Passive Verbs is nothing more than *aru* 'to be' and *eru* 'to get,' the literal meaning of *mirareru*, 'to be seen,' being 'get-be-see.' It is easy to see why the same form may also have a potential signification.

§ 74. OTHER DERIVATIVE VERBS.

Verbs are formed from nouns by adding various terminations as :—

Yadoru, to lodge,   from *yado*, a lodging.
Tsŭkamu, to grasp, from *tsuka*, a hilt.
Tsunagu, to tie,   from *tsuna*, a rope.
Utau, to sing,   from *uta*, song, poetry.

§ 75. Many Chinese and other uninflected words (which are really nouns) do duty as verbs with the help of the Japanese verb *suru* 'to do.' In most cases of this kind *suru* remains a distinct word, as *shimpai suru* 'to be anxious,' *hai suru* 'to abolish,' *riokō suru* 'to travel,' etc. But with some words *suru* in this position suffers a considerable change. The *s* takes the *nigori*, and becomes *j*, while the conjugation is assimilated to that of verbs of the second conjugation whose stem ends in *i*. Thus *kin*, a Chinese word which means 'prohibition,' forms with *suru* a verb *kinjiru* which is not conjugated like *suru* but like *dekiru*.

§ 76. Derivative verbs are formed from adjectives by adding *mu* to the stem. These verbs are intransitive, The corresponding transitive verbs add *meru* to the stem.

Examples.

Takamu, to become high, *takameru*, to make high, from *takai*, high.

Hiromu, to become wide, *hiromeru*, to spread abroad, from *hiroi*, wide.

Fujin	*no*	*chii*	*wo*	I think of raising the position of women.
woman		position		
takameyō	*to*	*omou.*		
make high		think		

§ 77. The schemes of conjugation given on pp. 44 to 49 are intended to show the formation of the simple moods and tenses of the verb, but there are many compound expressions in use as their equivalents. These are so numerous that it is impossible to give them all, but the following tables, which comprise a selection of the more common, may be useful. The Auxiliary Verbs used in these combinations are treated of in Chapter VIII.

It must not be supposed that the forms arranged under the same heading are used altogether indiscriminately. There are distinctions between them, some of which are pointed out in these pages and others will be learnt by practice.

THE VERB.

§ 78. ## CONJUGATION I.

Kasu, to lend.

Tense	Positive	Negative
	INDICATIVE MOOD.	
Present	Kasu Kasu no desŭ Kasu no da Kashimasŭ	Kasanŭ Kasanai Kasanai no desŭ Kasanai no da Kashimasenŭ
Past	Kashĭta Kashĭta no desŭ Kashimashĭta	Kasananda Kasanakatta Kashĭta no de nai Kasanakatta no desŭ Kasanai no deshĭta Kashimasenanda Kashĭmasenŭ d'atta
Perfect or Continuative*	Kashĭte oru or iru Kashĭte imasŭ	Kashĭte oranŭ or inai Kashĭte imasenŭ
Future	Kasō Kasu d'arō Kasu no deshō Kashimashō	Kasumai Kasanai d'arō Kasanai no deshō Kashimasŭmai
Probable Past	Kashĭtarō Kashĭta no deshō Kashimashĭtarō	Kasanandarō Kasanakattarō Kasanakatta no deshō Kashimasenandarō

* See below, § 100.

CONDITIONAL MOOD.

Tense	Positive	Negative
Present	*Kaseba*	*Kasaneba*
		Kasanŭ kereba
	Kasaba	*Kasazuba*
	Kasu to	*Kasanŭ to*
		Kasanai to
	Kasu nara	*Kasanŭ nara*
	Kasu toki wa	*Kasanŭ toki wa*
	Kashite wa	*Kasanakŭ te wa*
	Kashimasŭ to	*Kashimasenŭ to*
Past	*Kashitara*	*Kasanandara*
		Kasanakattara
	Kashita nara	*Kasananda nara*
		Kasanakatta nara
	Kashimashitara	*Kashimasenandara*
Perfect or Continuative	*Kashite iru nara*	*Kashite inai nara*

CONCESSIVE MOOD.

Tense	Positive	Negative
Present	*Kasedo*	*Kasanedo*
		Kasanakeredo
	Kasu keredo	*Kasanŭ keredo*
		Kasanai keredo
	Kasu to iyedo	*Kasanŭ to iyedo*
	Kashite mo	*Kasanŭ de mo*
	Kashimasŭ keredo	*Kashimasenŭ keredo*
Past	*Kashitaredo*	*Kasanandaredo*
	Kashita keredo	*Kasananda keredo*
		Kasanakatta keredo
	Kashitemo	*Kasanakŭ te mo*
	Kashimashita keredo	*Kashimasenanda keredo*
Perfect or Continuative	*Kashite oru keredo*	*Kashite inai keredo*
Future	*Kasu to mo*	*Kasanŭ to mo*
		Kasazu to mo

THE VERB.

IMPERATIVE MOOD.	
Positive	Negative
Kase	Kasuna
O kashi nasare	O kashi nasaruna
Kashite kure	Kashite kureruna
Kashi na	Kashi nasanna

PARTICIPLE.	
Positive	Negative
Kashīte	Kasazu
	Kasazu ni
	Kasanakū te
	Kasanai de..
Kashimashite	Kashimasezu
	Kashimasezu ni

ALTERNATIVE FORM.
Positive Kashītari; Negative Kasanandari.

DESIDERATIVE ADJECTIVE.
Positive Kashitai; Negative Kashītaku nai.

CAUSATIVE VERB.
Positive Kasaseru; Negative Kasasenū.

PASSIVE OR POTENTIAL VERB.
Positive Kasareru; Negative Kasarenū.

POTENTIAL VERB.
Positive Kaseru; Negative Kasenū.

§ 79. CONJUGATION II.

Taberu, to eat.

Tense	Positive	Negative
Present	*Taberu* *Taberu no desŭ* *Taberu no da* *Tabemasŭ*	*Tabenŭ* *Tabenai* *Tabenai no desŭ* *Tabenai no da* *Tabemasenŭ*
Past	*Tabeta* *Tabeta no desŭ* *Tabemashĭta*	*Tabenanda* *Tabenakatta* *Tabeta no de nai* *Tabenakatta no desŭ* *Tabenai no deshĭta* *Tabemasenanda* *Tabemasenŭ d'atta*
Perfect or Continuative*....	*Tabete oru* *Tabete iru* *Tabete imasŭ*	*Tabete oranŭ* *Tabete inai* *Tabete imasenŭ*
Future........	*Tabeyō* *Taberu d'arō* *Taberu no deshō* *Tabemashō*	*Tabemai* *Tabenai d'arō* *Tabenai no deshō* *Tabemasŭmai*
Probable Past ..	*Tabetarō* *Tabeta no deshō* *Tabemashĭtarō*	*Tabenandarō* *Tabenakattarō* *Tabenakatta no deshō* *Tabemasenand'arō*

* See below, § 100.

THE VERB. 91

CONDITIONAL MOOD.

Tense	Positive	Negative
Present	Tabereba Tabeba Taberu to Taberu nara Taberu toki wa Tabete wa Tabemasū to	Tabeneba Tabenūkereba Tabenakereba Tabezu-ba Tabenū to Tabenai to Tabenū nara Tabenū toki wa Tabenakū te wa Tabemasenū to
Past..........	Tabetara Tabeta nara Tabemashitara	Tabenandara Tabenakattara Tabenanda nara Tabenakatta nara Tabemasenandara
Perfect or Continuative	Tabete iru nara	Tabete inai nara

CONCESSIVE MOOD.

Tense	Positive	Negative
Present	Taberedo Taberu keredo Taberu to iyedo Tabe te mo Tabemasū keredo	Tabenedo Tabenakeredo Tabenūkeredo Tabenai keredo Tabenū to iyedo Tabenū de mo Tabemasenū keredo
Past..........	Tabetaredo Tabeta keredo Tabe te mo Tabemashita keredo	Tabenandaredo Tabenanda keredo Tabenakatta keredo Tabenakū te mo Tabemasenanda keredo
Perfect or Continuative	Tabete oru keredo	Tabete inai keredo
Future........	Taberu to mo	Tabenū to mo Tabezu to mo

IMPERATIVE MOOD.

Positive	Negative
Tabero	Taberuna.
O tabe* nasare	O tabe* nasaruna.
Tabete o kure	Tabete kureruna.
Tabe na	Tabe nasanna.

PARTICIPLE.

Positive	Negative
Tabete	Tabezu
	Tabezu ni
	Tabenakŭ te
	Tabenai de
Tabemashite	Tabemasezu
	Tabemasezu ni

* *O tabe nasare, o tabe nasaruna* are not used; *o agari nasare, o agari nasaruna* are used instead. They are simply given to show the usual form in other verbs of this conjugation.

ALTERNATIVE FORM.
Positive   *Tabetari;*   Negative   *Tabenandari.*

DESIDERATIVE ADJECTIVE.
Positive   *Tabetai;*   Negative   *Tabetaku nai.*

CAUSATIVE VERB.
Positive   *Tabesaseru;*   Negative   *Tabesasenŭ.*

PASSIVE OR POTENTIAL VERB.
Positive   *Taberareru;*   Negative   *Taberarenŭ.*

POTENTIAL VERB.
Wanting.

CHAPTER VII.

THE ADJECTIVE.

§ 80. The Adjective is conjugated as follows:—

HIROI WIDE

Stem	*Hiro*	Wide
Predicate, Adverb or Indefinite Form	*Hiroku* or *hirō* ...	Wide; widely
	hiroku te	being wide
	hiroku te wa	if wide
	hiroku te mo	even though wide
	hiroku ba or	
	hirokumba	if it should be wide
	hiroku nai	is not wide
	hirok'atta	was wide
	hirok'arō	will be wide
Attributive and Verbal Form..:..	*Hiroi*	Wide (before a noun); is wide
Conditional.........	*Hirokereba*	If it be wide
Concessive	*Hirokeredo*	Though it is or be wide
Abstract Noun.....	*Hirosa*	Width

A comparison of this conjugation with the conjugation of verbs will show that they are essentially identical. The stem of the verb corresponds to the stem of the adjective, and the Indefinite Form to the Adverbial Form. The Negative Base is not in use in the case of the Adjective, for Negative Forms or for the Future, but the Hypothetical Form is *hiroku ba* where the Adverbial Form stands for the Neg. Base. The Present Indicative of the Verb corresponds to the Verbal Form of the Adjective, and the Conditional and Concessive Forms contain a Conditional Base viz. *hirokere.*

THE ADJECTIVE.

§ 81. THE STEM. *Hiro*.

The Stem is used in forming compounds.

Thus from *naga* the stem of *nagai*, 'long,' and *saki*, 'a cape,' is derived *Nagasaki* (the literal signification of which is 'long cape'); from *yo* the stem of *yoi*, 'good,' and *sugiru*, 'to exceed,' we have the compound *yosugiru*, 'to be too good'; *usuguroi* 'dark-coloured,' is formed from *usu* stem of *usui*, 'thin,' and *kuroi*, 'black.'

Hadzukashi-sō na kawo de. shameful appearance face with	With a shamefaced expression of countenance.
Tegaru-sō ni iu keredo. hand light say although	Though he talks in an offhand manner.
Medzurashi-sō ni mite oru. curious looking is	He is looking at it as if it were a curious thing.

The stem occasionally stands by itself as a noun, as in the phrase *makkuro ni natta*, 'it has become quite black.'

§ 82. THE PREDICATE, ADVERB OR INDEFINITE FORM. *Hiroku* or *hirō*.

By adding *ku* to the stem we get the predicate, or form used where the verb 'to be' comes between the adjective and the noun. The same form is also used as an adverb.*

The contracted form *hirō* is obtained by dropping the *k* of *hiroku* and joining into one syllable the last vowel of the stem and the *u* of the termination. In this way, *hiroku* becomes first *hiroü* and then *hirō*; *hayaku* becomes successively *hayaü* and *hayō*; *shigeku*, 'dense,' loses first its *k* and becomes *shigeü*, which is then contracted into *shigyō*; *furuku* becomes *furū*. Adjectives whose adverbial form ends in *iku* lose the *k* but suffer no further change. Thus *yakamashiku*, 'noisy,' is contracted into *yakamashiu*.

---

* As in German.

As a predicate, the contracted form is better, but when used as an adverb, the uncontracted form is more usual, especially in the Tokio dialect.

Examples.

1. As a Predicate.

O hayō. (hon.) early	Good morning.
O hayō gozarimasŭ. (hon.) early are	Good morning (more polite).
Mada hayō gozarimasenŭ ka? yet early is not ?	Isn't it early yet?
Kono mŭma wa goku takō this horse very dear gozarimasŭ. is	This horse is very dear.

2. As an Adverb.

Hayaku or hayō!	Quick!
Hayaku o ide nasare! quickly come do	Come quickly. Come early.
Yoku dekita.	It is well made.
Shiroku nurimashita.	He painted it white.

3. As a Noun.

Osoku made hataraita. late until worked	He worked till late.
Ōku no hito ni numerous man shirasete. making known	Letting people in general know.

4. As Indefinite Form.

Rule. Whenever in English two or more adjectives are joined by the conjunction 'and,' all but the last take in Japanese the adverbial or indefinite form. Compare the rule given for the use of the Indefinite Form of verbs on p. 52.

Examples.

Kumo kuroku, ame hidoi. clouds black rain violent	The clouds are black and the rain is violent.
Kami no ke ga kuroku, me ga awoi onna. head hair black eyes blue woman	A woman with black hair and blue eyes.
Utsukushiku chisai kodomo. pretty little child	A pretty little child.
Oya mo naku kiōdai mo nai to iu mono da. parents not brothers or sisters even not called person is	He is a person who has neither parents nor brothers or sisters.
Dete kita no wa sono soma no niōbō to miyete, toshigoro wa nijiū shichi hachi de, iro shiroku, hana suji tōri, yamaga ni wa mare na onna de gozaimasŭ. having come out that woodcutter's wife seeming age twenty seven eight complexion white nose line was thorough mountain huts rare woman is	The person who came forth was apparently the woodcutter's wife. She was twenty seven or twenty eight years of age, with fair complexion and a straight nose, and was a style of woman not often found in mountain huts.

The last sentence shows that in this construction the adverbial forms of adjectives (*shiroku*) and the stems of verbs (*tōri*) are given the same syntactical value. In ordinary conversation some other construction is generally preferred.

§ 83. Adverb with *te*. *Hirokŭ te*.

Te in this combination may be taken as the equivalent of *atte*, 'being.'

Examples.

Kurakŭ te miyemasenŭ. dark being cannot see	It is so dark I cannot see.

THE ADJECTIVE. 97

Samukŭ te tamarimasenŭ. cold not endure	It is so cold I cannot endure it.
Isogashikŭ te tsui go busy casually (hon.) *busata wo itashimashita.* not giving news did	I have been so busy that I have somehow or another not come to see you.
Shirokŭ te yoroshi. being white is good	Its being white is an advantage.
Atsukŭ te hiroi.	It is thick and wide.

§ 84. Adverb with *te wa*. *Hirokŭ te wa*, commonly contracted into *hirokŭcha*.

This form is a sort of Conditional Mood. It is in very common use, especially with the Adverbial Form of the Negative Adjective.

Examples.

Hatsuka yori osokŭ te wa 20th than late *komaru.* am inconvenienced	I shall be inconvenienced if it is later than the twentieth.
Usukŭcha ikenai. thin does not do	It won't do for it to be too thin.
Nakŭcha naranŭ. if not does not become	I must have it.
Sugu ni kawanakŭcha at once not buying *narimasenŭ.* does not do	Some must be bought at once.

§ 84. Adverb with *te mo*. *Hirokŭ te mo*.
This is a Concessive Form. It belongs to no particular tense.

Donnani kitanakŭ te mo how much dirty *kamawanai.* don't care	I don't care how dirty it is.
Abunakŭ te mo kamau dangerous being even care *mono ka?* person ?	Who cares even if it is dangerous?

Usukŭ te mo daijōbu desŭ. It is quite safe, though it is
thin   safe   is thin.

§ 85. Adverb with *ba*. *Hirokuba* or *hirokumba*.

Ba with the Adverb corresponds to the Hypothetical Form of the Verb, and like it is not much used.

§ 86. The Negative of Adjectives is formed with the help of the Negative Adjectives *nai* 'is not,' and the past and future by adding the past and future of *aru* 'to be,' to the Adverbial form.

Examples.

Omoshirok' atta. It was amusing.

Mō osok' arō. It must be late.
already late will be

Akaku nai no wa iranai. I don't want any that are
red not   don't want   not red.

§ 87. THE ATTRIBUTIVE FORM. *Hiroi.*

This form may be obtained by adding *i* to the root. It is really, however, a contraction for an older form in *ki*, the *k* being omitted.*

This form is used when the adjective immediately precedes the noun.

Examples of Attributive Form.

Yoi hito. A good man.

Warui onna. A bad woman.

Atsui kami. Thick paper.

Awoi kawo. A pale face.

Samui koto! How cold it is! (lit. the cold thing!).

Fukai toki wa fune de wataru. If it is deep, I shall cross in
deep time   boat   cross   a boat.

---

* The older form is not quite obsolete. It is retained for example in the proverb *tori naki sato no kōmori,* 'the bat of No-bird-town,' and in the termination *beki.*

THE ADJECTIVE. 99

The particle *no* is often attached to this form of the adjective. *No* has in this position very much the force of the English indefinite pronoun 'one.' It is possibly here a contraction for *mono* 'thing.' This derivation would at any rate suit the meaning.

Examples.

Yoroshi no wa nai ka?	Have you no good ones?
Shiroi no bakari aru.	There are only white ones.
Kuroi no wa ikutsŭ arimasŭ? black how many	How many black ones are there?
Akai no hitotsŭ mo gozarima- red *senŭ.*	I have not a single red one.
Kore wa hiakŭshō no warui farmer bad *no de wa nai.*	This is not the farmer's fault.
Yori-dotte mo ii choose having taken even good *no desŭ ka?* is ?	May I have pick and choice?

No ni following this form of the adjective may be translated 'while,' as in the examples :—

Sono mama de ii no ni, naze that state good why *soto ye dashīta?* outside put-out	While they were well enough as they were, why did you put them out of doors?
Samui no ni naze atatakai ki- cold why warm *mono ki nai ka?* clothes wear not	Why don't you wear warm clothes in this cold weather?

This form of the adjective may stand by itself as a noun, as in the following examples :—

Sui mo amai mo shiri-nui- sour sweet know passed *ta hito desŭ.* through man is	He is a man who knows perfectly what is what.

100 THE ADJECTIVE.

Nagai mijikai mo iwazu ni Take receipt of the money with-
long short not-saying out making any fuss about it.
kane wo ukctore.
money receive

O kayeri nasatta hō ga yoroshī I think you had better go away.
return did side good
deshō.
will be

§ 88. THE VERBAL FORM. *Hiroi.*

The same form is used for the adjective combined with the substantive verb as for the attributive form. The older and book language has a special form for this, viz. *hiroshi*, produced by adding *shi* to the stem.*

Examples of the Verbal Form.

Amari mutsukashī. It is too difficult.
too is difficult

Kawa ga asai kara daijōbu da. It is quite safe because the
river shallow safe river is shallow.

Tenki wa yoroshī. The weather is good.

Mugi wo maite, kome no If we sow wheat, we never
wheat having sown rice have a crop of rice, and if we
dekita koto mo naku; mame wo sow beans we never have a crop
become beans of hemp.
maite, asa no hayeta koto mo
hemp grown thing also
nai.
is not

Warui to wa iwanai. I don't say that it is bad.

Osoi to ikenai. It wont do to be late.

§ 89. THE CONDITIONAL FORM. *Hirokereba.*

Kereba is often pronounced *kereya* or *keria.*

---

* In some phrases the old form is still in use, as *shōbu nashi* 'there is no victory-defeat,' 'neither side has won;' *kidzukai nashi*, 'there is no cause for alarm' *yoshi, yoshi*, lit. 'is good, is good,' 'all right—never mind!'

THE ADJECTIVE.

Examples.

Miōnichi tenki ga yoroshī-kereba, mairimasū. tomorrow weather if good come	I will come to-morrow, if the weather is good.
Hītori de ii-nikukereba, wata-kūshi wa go issho ni ikimashō. alone if say difficult I along with will go	If you find a difficulty in telling it all by yourself, I will go with you.
Michi no nukari ga hanahadashīkereba. road mud since extreme	As the mud of the road was something awful.
Miōnichi tsugō ga warukereba, asatte kimashō. tomorrow convenience if bad day after tomorrow will come	If tomorrow is not convenient, I will come the day after.

Other Conditional expressions are *hiroi toki wa*, *hiroku* (or *hirō*) *gozarimasureba*, *hiroi to*, *hiroi nara* and *hirokū te wa*. These have nearly the same meaning as *hirokereba* and are more common.

§ 90. THE CONCESSIVE FORM. *Hirokeredo*.

Hiroi keredo or *hirokū te mo* are generally preferred to *hirokeredo*.

Example.

Warukeredo, (better *warui keredo* or *warukū te mo*) *shikata ga nai*.	Though bad, it can't be helped.

§ 91. THE ABSTRACT NOUN. *Hirosa*.
See § 12.

DERIVATIVE ADJECTIVES.

§ 92. A number of Derivative Adjectives are formed from nouns by adding *rashī*, a termination which corresponds to the English 'ish' or 'ly.' Examples. *Kodomorashī*, 'childish,' *bakarashī*, 'foolish.'

§ 93. Desiderative Adjectives.

Adjectives may be formed from verbs by adding to the stem the termination *tai* which means 'desirous' or 'desirable.' The forms thus obtained are used where we should employ such verbs as 'wish' or 'want.'

Examples.

Moraitai mono.
receive like thing
A thing I should like to get a present of.

Ikitai.
I want to go.

Kaitai or *kaitō gozaimasŭ.*
I want to buy.

O hanashi wo (or *ga*) *shĭtai*
talk   wish to do
to omotte imasŭ.
thinking remain
I have been wanting to talk to you.

The Desiderative Adjective may take either *ga* or *wo* before it, as shown in the last example.

§ 94. Negative Adjectives.

An important class of adjectives is that which is formed from verbs by adding to the negative base the negative adjective *nai,* 'not.'

They are formed from all verbs, with a very few exceptions, and are constantly used to replace the negative forms of the verb proper.

The Predicate and Adverb of these adjectives is seldom contracted, and the Abstract Noun is not in use.

Examples.

Wakaranai.
it is unintelligible
I don't understand.

Ukeawanai.
I don't guarantee it.

Shiranai hito.
A man I don't know.

Yakanakŭ te mo yoroshi.
not roasting even is good
You need not roast it.

Kaze ga nai kara, ho wo wind not because sail *kaketemo kakenaku te mo onaji* set not set same *koto da.* thing is	It is all the same whether you hoist sail or not, as there is no wind.
Shiranakereba, sensaku shima- inquiry *shō.*	If he does not know, I will make inquiries.
Sonna koto wo iwana- that sort of thing if not *kereba ii no ni.* say good while	It would have been better if he had said nothing of the sort.
Mono wo mo iwanai de thing without saying *nigedashīta.* ran off	He ran off without saying a word.
Ikanakŭ te wa narimasenŭ. not-go if does not become	I must go.

In the idiom exemplified in the last sentence, the word *narimasenŭ* is often omitted, and *te wa* contracted into *cha*.

Examples.

Kawanakŭcha.	I must buy.
Te wo arawanakŭcha.	I must wash my hands.
Konakŭcha naranŭ.	He must come.

§. 95. *Beki.* This termination, which means 'ought,' 'should,' 'may,' 'must' or 'will,' is indispensable in all forms of the written language, but, by a curious caprice, it has been almost entirely banished from the colloquial. The uncontracted forms *beki* (attributive), *beku* (adverb) and *beshi* (adj. with substantive verb) are considered bookish and affected, while the contracted form *bei* is also condemned as characterizing the rustic dialect of the east of Japan. *Byō*, the contracted adverbial form, is seldom or never used except on the stage. In a few combinations, however, *beki, beku* remain in use, as *kō subeki hadzu da,* lit 'thus ought to do necessity is,' i.e. 'this is how it ought to be done,' *narubeku,* 'as far as possible,' *narubeku wa,* 'if possible.'. With verbs of the First Conjugation *beki* accompanies the Present Indicative, with verbs of the Second Conjugation, the stem, but in the latter case there is some confusion and the practice of the written language is sometimes followed.

On the whole, the student may be recommended not to trouble himself about *beki.*

§ 96. OTHER DERIVATIVE ADJECTIVES.

Katai 'hard,' *yasui* 'easy,' *nikui* 'difficult,' 'hateful,' are also added to the stems of verbs to form derivative adjectives.

Examples.

Ari-gatai.	It is difficult to be. (a phrase used to mean 'Thanks.')
Ii-nikui.	Difficult to say.
Mi-nikui.	Hateful to look at; ugly.
Koware-yasui.	Easy to break, fragile.

Other examples of derivative adjectives formed from verbs are *isogashī,* 'busy,' from *isogu,* 'to be in a hurry'; *osoroshī,* dreadful,' from *osoreru,* 'to fear.'

§ 97. Uninflected words used as Adjectives.

There are a number of nouns which do duty as adjectives, and are often considered as such. Like other nouns, they are properly speaking uninflected, but with the aid of certain particles, a conjugation may be made out for them corresponding to the conjugation of the adjective proper, as follows:—

THE ADJECTIVE.

Akiraka, Bright.

Stem	*Akiraka* ...	bright.
Predicate	*Akiraka de*	bright.
Adverb	*Akiraka ni*	brightly.
Attributive	*Akiraka na*	bright (before a noun).
Verbal Form	*Akiraka da*	is bright.
Conditional	*Akiraka nareba*	if bright.
Concessive	*Akiraka naredo*	though bright.
Abstract noun	*Akiraka na koto*	brightness.

Examples.

Rippa na mono ja nai ka ? Is it not grand?

Makoto ni o rippa de gozai- It is really splendid.
truly
masŭ.

Hi wa akiraka ni teru. The sun shines brightly.
sun   brightly   shines

Kinodoku na no wa Mori The one who is to be pitied
sorry   is Mr. Mori.
San da.

Bimbō ni natte iru kara Now that I have become poor,
poor   become because I must practise economy.
kenyaku shinakŭcha nari-
economy if-not-do   does
masenŭ.
not become

Are wa   ganko   na He is one of the old school—
he   obstinate prejudiced   an old fossil.
yatsu desŭ.
fellow

To this class of words belong *rippa* ' grand,' ' splendid : '
bimbō, ' poor ;' *kanemochi,* ' rich ; ' *kirei,* ' clean,' ' pretty,'
and a multitude of words of Chinese derivation.

Some adjectives proper use the termination *na* added to
the root as well as the regular attributive form.' Thus we
may say either *chisai* or *chisana,* ' small ;' *ōkī* or *ōkina,*

'big;' *okashi* or *okashina*, 'ridiculous.' English adjectives must often be translated in Japanese by other parts of speech. 'Single' for example is *hitoye no*, a noun with the possessive particle *no*; 'Japanese' is *Nippon no*, lit. 'of Japan;' 'fat' is *fŭtotta*, the past tense of a verb *fŭtoru* 'to get fat;' 'explicit' is *hakkiri shita*, an adverb followed by the past tense of *suru* 'to do.'

§ 98. DEGREES OF COMPARISON.—The Japanese adjective has no degrees of comparison. The idea of comparison is expressed in the following manner:—'the weather is finer today than yesterday' is in Japanese, *sakujitsŭ yori konnichi wa tenki ga yoroshi*. This is literally, 'than yesterday today the weather is good.'

Examples.

✓   *Watakŭshi yori anata o wakō gozaimasŭ.*
        I   than   you   young are   You are younger than I.

In sentences like this, the former part is often omitted if the meaning is clear without it, as *anata wa o wakō gozarimasŭ*, 'you are the younger,' or *anata no hō ga o wakō gozarimasŭ*, lit. ' your side is young.'

    Sore wa nawo yoroshiu gozarimasŭ.   That is still better.
     that   still   good   is

✓   *Mijikai hodo wa, yoroshi.*   The shorter the better.
       short   amount   is good

    Ane hodo ōkiku wa nai.   She is not so tall as her elder sister.
    elder sister   big   is not

    Omoi no hoka katai.   It is harder than I thought.
    thought   outside of   is hard

Instead of a Superlative Degree qualifying adverbs are used or the meaning is indicated by the context.

THE ADJECTIVE.

Examples.

   Kore wa ichiban takai.   This is the highest.
   this   No. 1   is high

✓   *Naka ni kore wa takai.*   This is the highest.
   among   this   is high

✓   *Mitsu no uchi ni sore wa*   That is the prettiest of the
   three   among   that   three.
ichiban kirei de gozaimasŭ.
No. 1   pretty   is

CHAPTER VIII.

AUXILIARY WORDS.

§ 99. *Aru*, 'to be,' 1st. conjugation. With the present indicative followed by the particle *de* and the verb *aru*, 'to be,' are formed a number of compound tenses which are in very common use. The present indicative is in this construction a noun and *de* the sign of the predicate. *De aru* is usually contracted into *da*, *de arō* into *d'arō*, etc.

Examples.

Itsu iku d'arō? when go will be	When is he likely to go?
Kore bakari de taranŭ this alone not suffice *d'arō.* will be	This alone won't be enough.
Konŭ d'atta. not come was	He did not come.
Yoroshiu arimasenŭ d'atta. good is not was	It was not good.

The last sentences show that the negative in this construction goes with the principal verb.

A similar construction is in use with adjectives.

Examples.

Katai da.	It is hard.
Atarashi de arimasenŭ.	It is not new.

The particle *no* often comes between the verb or adjective and *da*, *d'arō*, *d'atta* etc.

AUXILIARY WORDS. 109

Examples.

Konai no d'arō.	He is probably not coming.
Itsu iku no d'arō?	When is he going?
Mō chaku shimashīta no d'arō. already arrival did will be	He has probably arrived by this time.

When the verb *aru* preceded by *de*, the sign of the predicate, is followed by the polite termination *masŭ*, a still further contraction takes place, which is constantly used in familiar conversation. *De arimasŭ* is contracted into *demasŭ*, and then into *desŭ*, *de arimashō* into *demashō* and then into *deshō*, *de arimashīta* into *deshīta* etc.

The shorter and more contracted the phrase, the less polite it becomes. *Desŭ* is very much more familiar and less respectful than *de gozarimasŭ*.

Examples.

Sō desŭ.	It is so.
Dō desŭ ka?	How is it?

Gozaru and *gozarimasŭ* (in the Tokio dialect commonly pronounced *gozaimasŭ*), the polite substitutes for *aru*, may be used in the same way. *Gozaru* is not often heard in ordinary conversation.

Another series of compound tenses is formed by the past participle followed by *aru*.

Example.

Kite gozaimasŭ.	They have come.

The verbs *aru*, *arimasŭ*, *gozarimasŭ* may also be joined to the stem, as:—

Dochira ye o ide de gozarimasŭ ka? where go is	Where are you going?

§ 100. *Oru, iru,* 'to remain,' ' to dwell.'

With the various tenses of the verbs *oru* (1st. conj.) and *iru* (2nd. conj.) and the past participles of verbs are formed a series of tenses which in some verbs correspond to the compound tenses formed by the verb 'to be' and the present participle of English verbs; in others to the tenses formed by the verb 'to have' and the past participle.

In other words this combination has sometimes a Perfect, sometimes a Continuative Force.

For instance, *hataraite oru* means 'he is working' but *kite oru* means not 'he is coming,' but 'he has come.' *Iru* has the same meaning as *oru*. It usually forms a contraction with the verb, thus—*shitteru,* for *shitte iru,* 'I know' lit. 'having learnt, I remain.' The *kite gozarimasŭ* of the last section is slightly different in meaning from *kite. orimasŭ*. The former might be expanded into 'as they have come, there now are some;' the latter means 'they have come, and still remain.' Naturally the form with *oru* or *iru* is more in use in the case of living beings.

Examples.

Issaku nen no natsu kara keiko shite orimasŭ. before last year summer from study having made remain	I have been studying since the summer of the year before last.
Bakana koto wo itteru. foolish thing say remain	You are talking nonsense.
Kono tabi ni ana ga aite oru. these socks hole opened remains	These socks have got holes in them.
Dete orimasŭ.	He has gone out.
Tsuite orimasŭ.	It has arrived.

§ 101. *Naru,* 'to be.'

The verb *naru,* 'to be,' is extremely frequent in books.

In the spoken language it is most usually found in the Conditional Form as an auxiliary joined with the Indicative tenses of verbs. Thus it is common, instead of *ikeba*, 'if he goes,' to say, *iku nareba*, or *iku nara*;* for *ittareba* 'if he went' or 'had gone,' we may say *itta nareba* or *itta nara*. *Nara* may be used with adjectives in the same way, as *utsukushī nara* 'if pretty,' and is particularly frequent with those uninflected words described in § 97 which are used instead of adjectives. It has been already pointed out that the termination *na* of these words is a contraction for *naru*. *Naredo*, the Concessive Form, is also in use.

In the written and older language the present indicative of this verb was not *naru* but *nari*, and in some phrases this form is retained.

Example.

Tatoye kuchi yakūsoku nari	Granted that it is only a verbal promise.
suppose mouth promise	
to mo.	

Naru, 'to be,' should be distinguished from *naru*, 'to become.' The latter may be generally recognised by its being preceded by *ni* or *to*.

Examples.

Kirei ni naru.	To become beautiful.
Hito to naru.	To become a man.

§ 102. *Suru*, 'to do.' The conjugation of the irregular verb *suru* is given in § 44, and its use with the stems of verbs to form an emphatic negative has been explained in § 46. But perhaps the most common use of *suru* is to supply the place of verbal inflections in the case of Chinese and other words, which are themselves uninflected.

---

* *Nara* is merely a contraction for *nareba*. It is the *nara* which we have in the well-known phrase *sayō nara*, the literal meaning of which is 'if it be so,'='good bye.'

Examples.

Jisan suru.	To bring.
Undō suru.	To take exercise.
Sōdan shimashō.	I will consult (about it).
Shimpai suruna.	Don't be anxious.
Yōjin shinai to ikenai.	You must be careful.

For the honorific verb *nasaru*, the polite verb *masŭ* and the respectful verbs *itasu* and *mōsu*, see chapter XII.

§ 103. *Iu*, 'to say,' a regular verb of the first conjugation. It is used with other verbs in a way which will be understood from the following examples.

Aru to iu to.	If one say that there are, i.e. supposing that there are.
Aru to iyedomo.	Though one say that there are, i.e. granted that there are, although there are.
Iku to iu to.	If we say that we go i.e. if we go.
Tada naku to iu koto aru mono ka? simply cry called thing is ?	Who ever heard of anybody crying for nothing?

Iu used in this way is often altogether redundant.

§ 104. *Keru*, an old perfect of *kuru*, 'to come,' is much used in the Concessive Form *keredo* with the Indicative Tenses of verbs. In these combinations the meaning of the tense of the principal verb is not lost. *Itta keredo* for example means 'he went, but'—, while if one says *ikedo*, 'though go,' or *ittemo*, 'even having gone,' no particular tense is indicated.

Keredo is also used with the Verbal Form of Adjectives, as *nigai keredo*, 'though it is bitter.'

It may be useful to notice here some nouns which for want of a better name may be called Auxiliary Nouns.

§ 105. *Hadzu*, 'necessity,' 'obligation,' is much used to express the idea contained in our auxiliary verbs 'ought,' 'must.'

Examples.

Kono shina ga makoto ni yasui. this article truly is cheap	These articles are really cheap.
Hanahada warui kara, yasui hadzu da. very bad cheap necessity	They ought to be, for they are very bad.
Sakujitsu iku hadzu de arimashita. yesterday go was	He ought to have gone yesterday.
Danna wa konnichi o ide nasaru hadzu desŭ. master today is	Master ought to come (i.e. is expected) to-day.
Shirō hadzu wa nai. will know	There is no reason why he should know. He can't possibly find out.
Sonna koto wo shiranakatta yo. such did not know	I tell you I knew nothing of the kind.
Shiranai hadzu da. not know necessity is	How could you know?
Sakujitsu sono kane wo uketoru hadzu deshita. yesterday that money receive necessity was	I was to have been paid that money yesterday.
Raigetsu ikubeki hadzu desŭ. next month go ought necessity is	He is to go next month.

Iku hadzu will do as well as, or better than, *ikubeki hadzu* in the last sentence.

§ 106. *Koto*, 'action,' 'thing,' is much used with adjectives and the forms of verbs which are capable of being made adjectives in a way which will be best understood from a few examples:—

Iku koto.	The going.
Ikanŭ koto.	The not going.
Itta koto.	The having gone.
Iku koto wa dekimashō ka? going thing will be possible	Will it be possible to go?
Ikanŭ koto wa arumai. not going thing will not be	He will surely go.
Tōkiō ye itta koto arimasŭ ka? gone thing is	Has he ever gone to Tokio?
Nippon no sake wo nonda koto wa nai. Japanese drunk thing is not	I have never drunk Japanese sake.
Noboru koto wa noborare-masŭ; oriru koto wa mudzukashī. ascending thing can ascend coming down is difficult	So far as getting up is concerned, I can get up; it is the coming down that is difficult.
Tōkiō ye kita koto wa kimashīta. come thing	He has come to Tokio, so far as that goes.
Watakŭshi wa mō nagai koto wa arumai. I long will not be	I don't think I have long to live.
Rippana hito ni naru to iu koto wo shōchi shite iru. splendid become know	I know that he will turn out a splendid fellow.

In the last sentence, *koto* takes the place of the conjunction 'that.' The *to iu* is superfluous, as it often is in Japanese.

Ichido o me ni kakatta koto once eye hung *ga arimasü.*	I have once met you.
Mita koto ga nai.	I have never seen.
Miru koto ga dekinai.	I can't see.
A! nemui koto! sleepy	Ah! how sleepy I am!
Wakizashi no koto wo short sword about *kikō to omotta.* will hear thought	I thought of enquiring about the short swords.
Taikomochi to wa dare no jester who *koto da?* is	Whom do you mean by 'professional jester?'
Omaye no koto sa.	I mean you.
Wakaranū to wa anata no not understand your *koto.* thing	Talk of not understanding! it is you who don't understand.
Watakūshi no kita koto wa come *danna ye shirasete o kure.* master make known give	Let your master know that I have come.
Kono shomotsu no koto wa this book *O Kiyo san kara kikimashita.* from heard	I heard about this book from Miss O Kiyo.

§ 107. *Mono* means 'thing,' but it frequently occurs after verbs in idiomatic expressions to which this meaning affords little clue.

Examples.

A. *Are wa sen ni* she before *miyenakatta onna da.* not seen woman is	A. I never saw that woman before. B. Very likely; considering that she has come this year.
B. *Sō d'arō; are wa* thus will be she *kotoshi kara kitan'da mono.* this year from come is thing	

A. *Ano tokoro ye tabako-* that place tobacco *ire wo atsurayete oita ;* holder having ordered put *are wo totte ki na.* that having taken come B. *Are wa raigetsu jiu ni* that next month *nichi no yakūsoku da mono wo—* day promise	A. I ordered a tobacco-pouch from that place; go and fetch it. B. Well, considering that it was promised for the 12th of next month —(The sentence is left unfinished as so often happens in Japanese.)
Kamau mono ka ? care thing ?	What do I care ?
Komatta mono da.	It is very annoying.
Ikitai mon' desŭ keredo— like to go is although	I should like to go, but—

§ 108. *Tokoro*, 'place.'

The ordinary mode of rendering in Japanese the relative clauses of European languages has been already described in § 28, but in order to bring out the relative force more distinctly, the word *tokoro* is sometimes introduced, in imitation of a Chinese idiom. Thus instead of *iku hito*, 'the man who goes,' it is possible to say *iku tokoro no hito*, which means the same thing.

The relative force may be recognized in the following examples:—

Omaye no kinō hanashĭta you yesterday said *tokoro de wa.* place by	By what you said yesterday.
Kampuku ni tayenai admiration do not endure *tokoro da.*	It is a thing for which I cannot contain my admiration.
Kōgoro san wa dō suru how doing *tokoro wo mi-nasatta ?* place see did	What did you see Mr. Kogoro do ?

Tokoro after the indicative tenses of verbs has the force of our 'just,' as in the following examples:—

AUXILIARY WORDS. 117

Anata no uwasa wo shìte iru   We were just talking about you.
    report
tokoro d'atta.

Nan'da ka kore kara yomu   I am just going to read what
     read   it is.
tokoro da.

Tonari no hanashi wo   We are just listening to what
neighbour talk   they are saying next door.
kite iru tokoro da.
listening

Other examples of *tokoro*.

Tokoro ga, sono ban ni—   Well then, on that night—
    that night

Yonde mita tokoro ga—   Upon reading it—
reading seen place

Sayō mōshimashìta tokoro ga—   On my saying so—

A. *Sazo o yakamashiu goza-*   A. I am sure you must have
 surely noisy will   been disturbed by our noise. B.
rimashìtarō. B. *Yakamashi*   Far from it!
have been   noisy
dokoro ka?
place ?

A. *Watakùshi no tokoro ma-*   A. Would it be possible for
  my place as   you to bring it as far as my
de motte kite   place? B. Thank you; we
far as having taken having come   would do much more than send
kudasaru koto ga deki-   it. ('No trouble at all' we
 give thing will be pos-   should say.)
mashō ka? B. *Hei! arigatō*
sible ? thank you
gozarimasŭ; sashi-agemasŭ
    send up
dokoro de wa gozarimasenŭ.
place it is not

CHAPTER IX.

PARTICLES.

§ 109. Particles have very varied uses in Japanese. They serve instead of case and plural terminations, and are also used as prepositions* and conjunctions.

Many of the particles described in this chapter are really identical with some of the terminations of verbs and adjectives already noticed.

They are mostly found after nouns, but are also used with those parts of the verb and adjective which are nouns in syntax, and a few are joined to verbs in the indicative mood or to adjectives in the verbal form.

For convenience of reference they have been arranged alphabetically.

§ 110. *Dano.* *Dano* is a contraction for *de aru no.* It is used in enumerations, where it is desired to make each thing mentioned as distinct as possible. It is usually translated 'and', but this does not give the full force of this particle. It resembles not a little the alternative form of the verb, and like it is found in pairs.

Examples.

Kiō	*dano*	*asu*	*dano*	Saying that they were coming, now today, now tomorrow, they have not come.
to-day		to-morrow		
mairu to te,†	*kimasenŭ.*			
come		come not		

---

* As they come after the noun, postpositions would be the more correct term.
† For *to itte.*

PARTICLES. 119

Iya dano ō dano to itte, no yes saying *shinai no desŭ.* not do s	Saying at one time 'no' at another time 'yes', he nevertheless does not do it.
Ninsoku dano, daiku dano coolie carpenter *yaneya dano yonde,* tiler having called *shigoto wo sasemashita.* work caused to do	He sent for coolies, and for carpenters, and for tilers, and set them to work.

§ 111. *De.* *De* is a contraction for *nite.* With the various verbs for 'to be', it forms a series of contractions, as *da* for *de aru, desŭ* for *de arimasŭ, deshita* for *de arimashita, datta* for *de atta, darō* for *de arō* etc. *De wa* is contracted into *ja.*

De means 'with,' 'by,' 'by means of,' 'on account of,' 'at,' 'in,' as in the following examples :—

Zōkin de ita wo nugŭ. floorcloth board wipe	To wipe the boards with a cloth.
Oka de iku. land go	To go by land.
Kawase de kane wo bill of exchange money *okuru.* send.	To send money by means of a bill of exchange.
Wakaranai de komaru. understanding	I am bothered by his not understanding.
Heya wa hanahada fuketsŭ de room very dirty by *komarimasŭ.* am annoyed	It is an annoyance that the room is so dirty.
Gan ichi wa de kare wildgoose one that *kore iu wake de wa gozaimasenŭ.* say reason is not	It is not that it is worth making a fuss about one wildgoose.
Yashiki de sodachimashita.	I was brought up in a *yashiki.*

Gakkō de sonna koto wa　They know nothing of the kind
college at such　　　　　at the college.
ikkō shiranŭ.
wholly do not know

Kore de mina desŭ ka?　Is this all?
this with all is ?

Dō iu shidai de?　Under what circumstances?
what called order

De as the sign of the Predicate. When two nouns are joined together by the verb 'to be' *(aru, arimasŭ, gozarimasŭ)*, the latter affixes *de*.

Examples.

Watakŭshi wa kajiya de gozarimasŭ.　I am the blacksmith.
　　　　　　　blacksmith

Kono mushi wa tombo desŭ.　This insect is a dragon fly.
　　insect　　dragon fly

Uso da.　It is a lie.

Ī ja nai ka?　Is it not good? *i.e.*, are you not satisfied?

Tōkiō hen no yatsu wa jinjaku de (atte) ikenŭ.　The Tokio fellows are effeminate and therefore useless.
　　quarter　fellow
effeminate　not go

Neruson wa Igirisŭ no hĭto de (atte), kaigun no gōketsŭ desŭ.　Nelson was an Englishman and a naval hero.
Nelson　　Englishman
　　　　navy　　hero
is

Kore wa ō hiōban no mono de (atte), Aioi chō ni orimashĭta.　He had a great reputation, and lived in Aioi St.
He　great　report
　　　　　　street
lived

De as the mark of the predicate is much used in forming the compound tenses of verbs and adjectives. See § 99.

Demo combines the meaning of *de* with that of *mo* 'even,' 'also.' It may generally be translated 'even'.

Sayō demo gozai- thus (pred.) even it will *mashō ga,—* be but	That is probably even so, but—
Demo gozaimashō ga,—	(Same as last.)
Demo—	Yes, but—
Sore demo ikenai. that with even it can't go	Even so it won't do.
Ōkata taki ye demo probably waterfall to *mawatta no de gozarimashō.* gone round will be	He has probably gone round to the waterfall. (*Demo* here shows that the remark is a mere guess.)
Ato demo yoroshī. after even is good	It will do afterwards.
Sore wa kodomo demo wakaru. that child even is in- telligible	Even a child understands that.
Fŭtotta no demo, yaseta no fat lean *demo yoroshī.* is good	Either fat ones or lean ones will do.
Seiyō no hĭto demo west ocean man *Shinajin demo nai.* Chinese	He is neither a European nor a Chinaman.

In the last sentence we have a combination of *de* as predicate and *mo*, repeated with two nouns in the sense of 'both.'

For *demo* with Interrogative Pronouns see § 26.

§ 112. *Dzutsu*, 'each;' 'every,' 'apiece'.

Examples.

Kono kusuri wa ichi nichi this medicine one day *sando dzutsu nomu no* three times each drink *desŭ.* is	This medicine is taken three times every day.

Hitori dzutsu hairima-shita. one person at a time entered	They came in one at a time.
Toshi ni nido gurai dzutsu Tōkiō ye dete kuru wake ni wa ikumai ka? year twice amount out come reason will not go?	Would it not be possible to come to Tokio twice every year?
Mina ni fŭtatsu dzutsu haitte oru. all two each	There are two in each of them.

§ 113. *Ga.* *Ga* was originally a possessive particle, and it still retains this force in certain phrases.

Examples.

Koma-ga-take.	Colt's peak (the name of a mountain).
Jiu nen ga aida. ten year space	For the space of ten years. (*jiu nen no aida* is equally good and much more common.)
Ore ga me no maye de saye. my eyes before even	Before my very eyes.
Kore ga tame ni.	On this account.
Waga kuni.	One's country.
Waga kiōdai.	One's own brothers and sisters.

It is better not to use *ga* as a possessive particle except in phrases for which there is good precedent.

By the process described in § 65 *ga* has in the modern colloquial come to be chiefly used as the sign of the nominative case. This case is, however, not necessarily accompanied by *ga*. It is omitted when *wa* or *mo* follows the noun and in many other cases, and a noun may be in the nominative case without any particle at all being added. *Ga* is almost always used before the verbs *aru* 'to be,' *dekiru* 'to become,' 'to be made,' and *oru* and *iru* 'to remain.'

Examples of *ga* as sign of the nominative case.

+ ʎ *Kane ga aru ka?* — Is there any money? Have you
money is ?   any money?

Hana ga takaku natta. — He gave himself airs.
nose high became

Isogu koto ga aru kara. — Because there is hurry.
hurry   is because

Sei ga takai hito. — A man of tall stature.
stature tall man

Shikata ga nai. — There is nothing to be done.
do-side is not   There is no help for it.

Uso ga arawareta. — Your falsehood has been found out.
falsehood has been revealed

Damatte iru hō ga — You had better hold your tongue.
being silent remain side
ii.
is good.

Saku ya hitogoroshi ga atta. — There was a murder last night.
last night murder was

Yūbe ame ga futta. — It rained last night.
last night rain fell

Ano sumiya san wa o kamisan ga arimasŭ ka? — Has that charcoal-dealer a wife?
that charcoal-dealer wife is ?

Aka ga nijittan aru. — There are twenty pieces of the red.
red twenty pieces

Oi-oi o hanashi ga nakaba ni narimasŭ kara, kore kara ga omoshiroku narimasŭ. — Now that we are at length getting to the middle of the story, what remains becomes interesting.
gradually story middle
becomes because this after
amusing becomes

O cha ga dekimashita. — The tea is ready.
(hon.) tea is made

Hima ga nakatta. — I had not time.
leisure was not

Yō ga aru kara, kochi o ide. — Come here; I've something for you to do.
business is because hither

The noun is often followed by *ga* where we should expect to find an accusative case, as in the following examples.

Kono imi ga wakarima- I don't understand the meaning
this meaning is unintelligi- of this.
senŭ.
ble

Hana ga o suki desŭ ka? Are you fond of flowers?
flower   like is ?

Kane ga uketoritai When you want to receive the
money   desirable to receive money.
toki wa.
time

Hanshō no oto ga suru. There is the firebell.
fire-bell   sound does

In the above sentences *imi, hana, kane,* and *oto* are regarded by the Japanese as the subjects of the verb or adjective which follows.

Ga, after those parts of adjectives and verbs which are used as nouns for purposes of syntax, has the same force as when it follows ordinary nouns.

Examples.

Iku   ga yoroshi.   You had better go.
the going   is good

Itta   ga yok'atta. He would have done better to
having gone   was good   have gone.

Yenrio   sezu   ni   You had better make no cere-
ceremony not doing   mony, but speak out frankly.
uchi-akete   hanashita   ga
frankly   the having spoken
yoroshi.
is good

Ori-ai   ga tsukimasenŭ. They don't hit it off together.
bend-meet   not hit.

Sugu   ni   tsurete   You should have brought him
at once   accompanying   here at once.
kita ga   ii.
the having come was good.

O ai ga nakū te yoroshiu   You need not meet him.
meet   without   good
gozaimasū.

Ga after a verb in the indicative mood or an adjective in the verbal form may generally be translated by 'but.' **YET** Sometimes a pause in speaking is a sufficient equivalent.

Examples.

Tori-naosō   to omou ga,   I wish to put it right, but I can't.
take will mend   think
tori-naosenai.
take cannot mend

Shinsetsu wa arigatai ga,   You are very kind, but I must
kindness   thanks   positively be going (to an inferior).
zehi   ikaneba naranai.
positively   if not go does not
become

Momen de wa arimasū ga,   It is true that they are cotton,
cotton (pred.)   is   but they have just been washed
aratte shitate-naoshīta bakari   and made up again.
washed made up renewed only
desū.
are

Senkoku nani ka miseru   You said awhile ago that you
former hour something show   had something to show me—may
mono ga aru to osshaimashīta   I look at it here?
thing is   said
ga, koko de haiken shitemo
here   see   having done
yoi no de gozarimasū ka?
good   is it

Ame ga ii kagen ni   If the rain would stop in reason-
rain   good condition   able time, it would be a good
yameba, yoroshi ga—   thing, but—(I don't expect it will).
if stop is good

After *tokoro, ga* has a somewhat similar force.

Kiite   mita tokoro ga.   Upon making inquiries—(a
having heard seen place   pause)

Tokoro ga or *daga* (for *de aru ga*) at the beginning of a sentence means 'this being so,' 'upon this,' 'well then.'

§ 114. *Gena* is found after verbs in the sense 'it would appear that,' 'I am told that,' 'I understand that.'

Examples.

Chūman to yara de gozari- dropsy ? is *masŭ gena.*	I am told that it is dropsy, if that is the right name.
Sakujitsŭ kayerimashĭta gena.	I understand that he came back yesterday.

Sō desŭ is commoner in Tokio than *gena*, which is more a Kioto expression, and has the same meaning. Ex. *Sakujitsu kayerimashĭta sō desŭ,* 'I understand that he returned yesterday.'

§ 115. *Ka* asks a question or intimates a doubt. it is very accurately represented by the mark of interrogation.

Examples.

Oki fune ka? large ship ?	Is it a large ship?
Watakŭshi ka?	Is it I?
Kita ka?	Has he come?

Ka between two nouns represents our conjunction 'or.'

Examples.

Osaka ka Nagasaki no uchi one or *ni orimasŭ.* other lives	He lives in one of the two places, Osaka or Nagasaki (I don't know which).
Ya ka tama ni atatte arrow bullet striking *shinimashĭta.* died	He was killed by an arrow or a bullet.
Otoko ka onna ka? man ? woman ?	Is it a male or a female?
Itta ka ikanai ka? has gone ? does not go ?	Has he gone, or not?

PARTICLES.

Sono hon no hiyōshi wa that book cover *atsui ka usui ka?* thick thin	Is the cover of that book thick or thin?

Where the clause begins with another interrogative word, *ka* may be omitted.

Example.

Dare desŭ?	Who is it?

The Japanese language having no special forms for indirect narration, a question or doubt when repeated in an indirect clause does not change its form as it does in English.

Examples.

Anata wa miōnichi iyo-iyo you tomorrow still *o ide nasaru ka to* do you come? (sign of quotation) *kiki ni kimashĭta.* hear to came	He came to enquire whether you had not changed your mind about going tomorrow.
Mŭma ka ushi ka shiranŭ. horse bull	I don't know whether it is a horse or a bull.
Donata ka to omoimashĭta. who I thought	I wondered who it was.
Ikō to omou. will go think	I am thinking of going.
Ikō ka to omou. will go? think	I think I may perhaps go.
Man - ichi sō iu koto 10,000 I so called *demo ari wa semai ka to* even be will not do? *omotta.* thought	It occurred to me whether there might not possibly be something of that kind.
Shijiu hak-ku ni narō forty eight nine will become *ka to omou kojiki.* think beggar	A beggar who one would think might be perhaps forty eight or forty nine years of age.
Aru ka mo shiremasenŭ. are? even can't know	There may be some, for aught I know.

PARTICLES.

For *ka* with Interrogative Pronouns see § 26.

§ 116. *Kara*, (with nouns) 'from,' 'since;' (with verbs) 'because,' 'after.'

Examples.
1. With nouns.

Konnichi kara.	From today.
Kore kara hachi ri.	Eight ri from here.
Saki kara.	From a while ago.
Doko kara ikimasŭ ka? where from go ?	By which way do you go?
Nakasendō kara ikimasŭ.	I am going by the Nakasendo.
Kanada kara seiyō ye from west ocean *ikō to zonjimasŭ.* will go think	I think of going to Europe viâ Canada.
Sore kara no koto ni shō that after thing will make *ja nai ka?* is not ?	Let us take it after that.
Kore kara.	Henceforth.
Omote no hō kara irete front side from having let in *kureruna.* don't give	Don't let him in by the front.
Kakushi kara kane wo pocket from money *dashīte.* taking out	Taking money from his pocket.
Ima kara sugu ni kayeru. now from immediately return	I am now going straight back again.

2. With Verbs.
(a). With Indicatives.

Oyaji ga naku narimashīta
father not became
kara ni san nichi o itoma
because two three day leave
wo negaimasŭ.
request

My father is dead, so I would ask you for two or three days leave.

Daijōbu desŭ kara, go safe is because *anshin—* easy-mind	You may make your mind at ease; it is quite safe.
Kono uchi no maye wa this house before *kuruma wo okasenai kara,* jinrikisha not-let-put because *sō omotte iro.* so thinking remain	Remember that I don't allow jinrikshas to be set down before this house.
Ima ni kayeru kara, now go back because *giosha ni sō itte o kure.* driver having said give	Tell the driver I am going away in a moment.

In the last two sentences *kara* is used where we might have expected *to*, the sign of quotation.

Atsui kara.	Because it is hot.

(b). With Past Participle.

Mama demo kutte boiled rice even having eaten *kara yok'arō.* after will be good	It will do after you have had your rice (to persons much inferior in rank).
Mina atsumatte kara all having assembled after *ni nasaremasenŭ ka?* not do	Won't you wait till they are all assembled before doing it?
Hiru-meshi wo tabete noon meal having eaten *kara de nakŭcha ikimasenŭ.* after if not don't go	I won't go till after I have had my midday meal.

§ 117. *Koso* is a very emphatic particle. It formerly had the effect of making the verb or adjective at the end of the sentence be put in the Conditional Base, and rare cases of the application of this rule are still met with.

Examples of *Koso*.

Omaye koso usotsuki da. you liar are	It is *you* who are the liar.

130   PARTICLES.

    Yū koso oide nasatta.　　　You are most welcome.
    well   come

    Watakŭshi koso go busata—　It is I who have neglected call-
    I   not-giving news　ing on you.

    Shinzŭreba koso, go chiukoku　It is just because I believe it,
    since believe   advice　that I offer you advice.
mōshimasŭ.
say (respectful)

    Yoroshi; sore de koso kimi　Right! *That* is like yourself.
    is good that with   you
da.
is

§ 118. *Made*, from *ma* 'space' and *de* 'with,' means 'to,' 'up to,' 'till,' 'until,' 'as far as,' 'inclusive of.'

Examples.

    Miōnichi made.　　　　　Till to-morrow.

    Yokohama kara Tōkiō made.　From Yokohama to Tokio.

    Hachiōji made donogurai　How far is it to Hachoji?
                   what quantity
aru?

    Iu made mo nai.　　　　It is not worth mentioning.
    saying as far as even is not

    Miōgonichi   made ni　It will be finished by the day
    day after tomorrow by　　after tomorrow.
deki-agarimasŭ.
is finished

    Kojiki to made ni natta.　He fell so low as to become a
    beggar as far as became　beggar.

    Namaye   made　　　　I even told you my name.
    name   as far as
o hanashi mōshĭta.
told

    Konnichi no hĭto ni made.　Even down to the men of this
    today   man   down to　day.

    Sakuban osoku made　　He had not returned up till late
    last night late until　　last night.
kayeranauda.
returned not

Doko made mo chikara wo tsūkushite. where as far as even strength having exhausted	Exerting one's strength to the very utmost.
Omaye made watashi wo ijimeru. you inclusive of me vex	Even you join in vexing me.

§ 119. *Mo* means 'also,' 'too,' 'even,' and, when repeated with two nouns, 'both.' It is the opposite of *wa*, *wa* meaning 'this, and nothing more,' 'this, if nothing more,' while *mo* implies that some thing else is associated with the noun to which it belongs. These two particles are therefore not found together. The case particles come before *mo*, but when it is used, *ga* (as sign of the nominative) and *wo* are generally omitted.

For *demo* see § 111.

It is the same particle which is used with the concessive form of verbs and with participles.

Examples.

1. With nouns.

Kono tsubo mo o kai nasare. this vase buy do	Buy this vase too.
Inu mo neko mo. dog cat	Both dogs and cats.
Ingirisŭ mo Nippon mo.	Both England and Japan.
Futatsu to mo.	Both of them.
Sō omou mo muri wa nai. so think even wrong is not	You are not wrong to think so.
Shiri mo shinai hito no tokoro ye tegami wo dashite. know do not man place letter sending off	Sending off a letter to a man she knows nothing of.

Omou and *shiri* in the last two sentences must be taken as nouns.

Shinkō shinai hito mo aru. There are some who do not
belief do not men also are believe.

2. With Verbs. ('even'). [*perhaps*]

Kuru ka mo shiranŭ. He may come, for aught I know.
come ? even don't know

This phrase implies a slight leaning to the opinion that he will come; *kuru ka shiranŭ* is simply an expression of ignorance.

Kiō wa mata Hāyaji I don't know whether that
today again fellow Hayaji may not come again
me ga koyō mo today.
(contemptuous termination) will come even
shirenŭ.
can't know

Tatoye nani to iwō to No matter what he may say,
supposing what will say the best plan is to take no notice
mo, tori-awanai no ga of him.
even take-meet-not
ichiban da.
no. 1 is

Mina tabenakŭ te mo You need not eat them all.
all not eating even
yoroshī.
is good

Aru keredo mo omaye I have some, but I won't give
are although even you you any.
ni wa yaranai.
to not give

§ 120. *Nagara*, 'whilst.'

1. With nouns.

Kage nagara. In my inmost heart.
shade

Go mendō nagara. I am sorry to trouble you, but—
trouble

Shikkei nagara. It is very rude of me, but—
impolite

Futatsu nagara. Both of them. The two of
two them.

PARTICLES.

2. With Verbs (stem form).

Utare nagara, kanjō wo shĭte. being beaten counting doing	Going on with his counting all the time he was being beaten.
Cha wo nomi nagara shabette orimashĭta. tea drink whilst chattering remained	They were chattering over their tea.
Kiusoku shi nagara. rest do	While resting.
O kotoba o damashi asobasu to shiri nagara mo. words (hon.) deceive condescend to know even	Even knowing all the time that your words were deceiving (highly respectful).
Osore nagara. fear	With all due respect.
Habakari nagara. fear	With all due respect.

§ 121. *Ni.* With nouns *ni* usually means 'to,' 'in,' 'at,' 'into,' 'on.'

Examples.

Kiōto ni iku. to go	He goes to Kioto.
Kiōto ni orimasŭ.	He lives in Kioto.
Uchi ni orimasŭ. within	He is at home.
Denshinkyoku ni haitta. telegraph office into entered	He went into the telegraph office.
Yengawa ni dashĭte oke. verandah on having put out put	Put it out on the verandah.
Kiuji ni mairi-mashĭta. waiting at table have come	I have come to wait at table.
Hito wo baka ni suru. person fool into make	To make a fool of a person.

Other meanings of *ni*.

Dare ni kiita? whom from did hear	From whom did you hear it?
Wakai toki, haha ni wakarete. young time mother from separated	Separated from her mother when young.
Toshi ni wa ōkī. year for is big	He is big for his age.
Anohito ni medzurashī chikoku desū. that man for rare late-hour is	It is very unusual for him to be so late.
Sore ni sōi nai. that about mistake is not	There is no mistake about that.
Sore ni, mata itte mireba— that in addition to again having gone when I saw.	And besides, when I went again to see—
Bekon ni tamago. bacon in addition to eggs.	Bacon and eggs.
Take ni suzume. bamboo sparrow	Bamboos and sparrows (as a subject of a painting).
Taisetsu na kushi kanzashi ni irui mo haitte imashita. valuable comb hairpin clothing having entered was	It contained clothing besides valuable combs and hairpins.
Yome ni ikitai. bride as wishes to go	She wants to get married.

Ni is often required in Japanese where there is no preposition in English.

Examples.

Isha ni sōdan suru. doctor consultation do	To consult a doctor.
Isha ni mite morau. having seen receive	To get a doctor to examine one.

PARTICLES. 135

Yotsu tsuji de
four crossroads at
basha ni aimashita.
carriage met

I met the carriage at the crossroads.

Mina ni ichi mai dzutsu
all one (flat object) apiece
yare.
give

Give them all one apiece.

Shindai - kagiri ni natta.
property-limit became

He became bankrupt.

Fuji san ni nobotta.
Fuji M! ascended

He ascended M! Fuji.

Tonari ni arimasu.

It is next door.

Ni with nouns often forms Adverbs.

Examples.

Makoto ni.
truth in

Truly.

Tashika ni.
certainty in

Certainly.

Dai ichi ni.
number one in

Firstly.

Uye ni.

Above.

Mare ni.

Seldom.

Before passive verbs, *ni* means 'by,' and before causative verbs indicates the person who is caused to perform the action.

Examples.

Hiyoko wa karasu ni
young chicken crow by
torareta.
was taken

The chicken was carried off by a crow.

Nani ka Moriyama ni mo
something by too
iwareta.
was said

He was talked to a little by Moriyama too.

Niwatori ni ye wo   Give the fowls their food.
fowl   food
kuwasero.
make eat

A similar construction is in use with some intransitive verbs.

Example.

Kono atsusa ni dōmo   I am knocked up by this heat.
this heat by somehow
 yowatta.
have become weak

Ni may follow those parts of the verb and adjective which are capable of becoming nouns.

(a) After Indicatives.

Tanoshimi ni omoimashita ni.   Whilst I was looking forward
pleasure as thought in   to it with pleasure.

Ashita tattara   When it would do quite well if
tomorrow if started   you started tomorrow, why insist
yok'arō ni naze shiite   (on going) today?
will be good in why persistently
konnichi—
today

Ame ga fureba, nureru to   When you knew very well that
rain if falls get wet   when (or if) it rains, people get
iu koto wa shirete   wet—(why did you go out in it?).
called thing being known
iru ni—
is in

Kike to iu ni—   When I tell you to listen—(why
listen say when   don't you listen?)

(b) After Adjectives.

Atsui ni komaru.   I am bothered by the heat.
being hot by am annoyed

Kurai no ni, naze chōchin   When it is so dark, why don't
being dark in why lantern   you bring a lantern?
wo motte konai?
taking not come

PARTICLES. 137

Yō   mo nai   ni   saki ye   As I have nothing for you to
business not while first   do, you may go to bed without
nereba   yoi.   waiting for me.
if go to bed is good

Ni is frequently found after *nashi*, the old verbal form of *nai* 'not,' as *yenrio nashi ni* 'without ceremony.' This is an ungrammatical construction but it has the sanction of use.

(c) After Stems.

Kimono wo arai ni yatta.   He sent the clothes to be
clothes   wash   sent   washed.

Naoshi ni yatta ka?   Did you send them to be
mend   sent   mended?

Mi ni itta.   He went to see.

It is not every verb with which this construction is usual or possible.

O kiki ni iremasū.   I will tell you (very respectful).
  hearing   put in

(d) After Negative Participles.

(*Gozen no*) *Ato no katadzuke*   He went to bed without putting
  meal   after putting away   away the (dinner) things.
wo sezu ni   nete
not doing   having gone to bed
shimaimashīta.
finished.

Kanjo wo harawazu ni   He never paid the bill after
bill   not paying   all.
shimaimashīta.
finished.

§ 122. *No* 'of' is the ordinary sign of the possessive case.

Examples.

Hito no ashi.   A man's leg.
Hako no kagi.   The key of the box.
Omaye no kimono.   Your clothes.

PARTICLES.

Ima no (itta koto) wa now of said thing *jōdan desŭ yo.* joke is (emph. part).	What I said just now was a joke, I tell you.
Sei no takai heitai. growth of high soldier	A tall soldier.
Yama no ōi kuni. mountain numerous country	A mountainous country.
Hi no aru uchi ni. sun's being within	While there is still daylight.
Rondon kara no dempō. London from telegram.	A telegram from London.
Kin no kahei.	Gold coins.
Miya no shĭta ni Shinto temple of below *yadoya ga niken aru.* inn two there are.	There are two inns below the Shinto temple.
Yane no uye kara tonde roof of above from flying *itte shimatta.* going finished	It flew away over the roof.
Me no maye de. eye of before at	Before my eyes.

No joins two words which relate to the same person or thing.

Dokushin no watakŭshi. single body	I, who am a single man.
Sagami no kuni.	The province of Sagami.
Mekura no kojiki. eye-dark of beggar.	A blind beggar.
Bettō no Tsunekichi.	The horse boy Tsunekichi.
Sugu ni koi to no at once come *kotodzuke.* message	A message that he was to come at once.

No is sometimes used like *dano* (which is $= da + no$) in enumerations. Here it may be rendered 'and' or 'or.'

PARTICLES.   139

Muko no yōshi no	Even if I asked for a thing so far
son-in-law adopted son	above my station as to become
to sonna mi ni sugita	your son-in-law or your adopted
such person exceeding	son, my request could not be
koto wa negatte mo	granted.
thing having requested even	
kanaimasenū.	
cannot be granted	

Moto yori izon no	Of course there is no difference
origin from difference of opinion	of opinion or anything of that kind.
nan'no to iu wake wa	
anything called reason	
nai.	
is not	

No with numerals.

| *Mitsu no hako.* | Three boxes. |
| *Sannin no dorobō.* | Three thieves. |

No after adjectives may very often be taken as equal to *mono* 'thing' and translated by 'one.'

Ito no futoi no wo motte	Bring me a stout piece of thread.
thread thick taking	
koi.	
come	

Kore! nibui no bakari aru;	Look here! there are only blunt
this blunt only are	ones. Are there no sharp ones?
togatta no ga arimasenū ka?	
sharp are not ?	

| *Ichiban yasui no no nedan.* | The price of the cheapest ones. |
| no. 1   cheap   price | |

Omaye wa warui no ni	You were certainly to blame.
you bad	
chigai nai.	
mistake	

In the following examples *no ni* may be rendered 'whilst.'

Ka ga ōi no	With such a lot of mosquitoes
mosquitoes numerous	about, why did you not put up the
ni naze kaya wo	musquito net?
whilst why mosquito net	
tsutte okanai?	
having hung not put	

140   PARTICLES.

Kiō wa Doyōbi de nai no today Saturday not *ni dōshite o ide* whilst how having done come *nasatta?* did	How is it you have come to-day? It is not Saturday.

No with verbs.

Keisatsusho ye police station to *tsurete iku no wa mendō* accompany going trouble *da kara.* is because	Because it is too much trouble to go with you to the police station.
Kō kaite arimasŭ no wo thus written is *mite.* seeing	Seeing what was thus written.
Omaye ga kowashĭta no ka? you broke ?	Is it of your breaking? Was it you who broke it?
Kowashĭta no wa watakŭshi broke I *de gozarimasenŭ.* is not	It was not I who broke it.
Kowasu no wo mita yo. break saw	I tell you I saw you break it.
Hisashī koto yenzetsu ga long thing speech *nakatta no ni, kiō wa* was not whilst to day *ichi ni nin no jōzu no* one two men clever *namaye ga miyeru.* names are visible	There have been no speeches for a long time but one or two clever speakers' names appear (on the list for) today.
Watakŭshi wa ima mita I now looked *no ni nani mo inai.* when something is not	When I looked just now, there was nothing there.
Doko ye o ide nasatta where to go did *no deshō? Ima made koko* will be now until here *ni o ide nasatta no ni.*	Where can he have gone to? He was here till a moment ago.

§ 123. *Ra* is a plural particle.

With adverbs of place *ra* adds vagueness to their meaning like the English 'abouts' in the same position. *Koko*, for example, means 'here,' *kokora* 'hereabouts.'

When it is wished to show respect *ra* is not used with nouns or pronouns, but *dachi* or *gata*.

Examples.

Sōzōshī yatsu ra da! noisy fellow (plural) is	What a noisy lot of fellows!
Sore ra no koto wo that (plural) thing *segare kara kikimashīta.* son from heard	I heard about (*koto*) those things from my son.
Go riokwan wa travel-residence *dochira desŭ?* whereabouts is	Whereabouts are your lodgings?

§ 124. *Sa* is found after nouns at the end of a sentence, where it has the same meaning as *da* 'is,' but is more emphatic.

Examples.

Ayashimu ni taranŭ think strange is not enough *wake sa.* reason is	There is not enough reason for thinking it strange.
Go sōdan mōsu consultation do *tsumori sa.* intention is	I intend to consult you.
Yō ga aru to sa. business is	He says there is something for you to do.
Sugu ni tonde iku no at once flying go *desŭ to sa.* is	I tell you it is said that it goes flying off at once.

Are sa.   (A phrase used as the equivalent
it is   of our 'I say' in calling one's atten-
                 tion or by way of remonstrance.)

Sayō sa.   Yes.
thus

§ 125. *Saye* after nouns or the stems of verbs means 'only.'

Examples.

Danna saye yoroshikereba,	If my master is only satisfied, I don't mind.
master only if is good	
watakŭshi wa dōdemo	
I anyhow	
yoroshiu gozarimasŭ.	
good is	
Yūdachi no maye ni	If they have only started before the shower.
shower before	
dekakete saye ireba.	
having gone out if remain	
Jibun ga hōritsu wo okashi	For my own part, so long as I don't break the law, there is no reason why I should be the least afraid of the police.
self law break	
saye senya (for *seneba*)	
only if not do	
nani mo junsa no kowai	
anything police afraid	
koto wa nai hadzu sa.	
thing not necessity	

De sometimes comes between the noun and *saye*. It adds nothing to the meaning.

Sempō de saye go shōchi	If the other party only agrees.
other party consent	
de gozarimasŭ nara.	
is if	
Chikŭshō de saye mo on wo	The very beasts have a sense of gratitude.
beast favour	
shiru.	
know	

§ 126. *Shi* is used with verbs in the indicative mood as a conjunction. It may be rendered 'and,' 'and also,' 'not only—but,' 'and so.'

PARTICLES. 143

Examples.

Michi mo yohodo aru shi, way much is *osoku natteru kara,* late has become because *hito ban koko ni tomatte,* one night here having stayed *ashita tattara yok'arō.* tomorrow if started will be good	As you have a long way to go, and besides it has got late, you had better stay here for one night, and start tomorrow.
Tōi michi demo ari wa distant way even be *shimai shi, hashi wo* will not do bridge *watareba tsui hana no* if cross casually nose *saki.* before	Not only is it no great way off, but if you cross the bridge, there it is before your nose.
Soto wo arukeba ashi ga outside if walk leg *kutabireru shi, uchi ni* get tired at home *oreba taikutsu suru shi,* if remain ennui do *jitsu ni dōmo—* truly somehow	If I go out, my legs get tired, and if I stay at home I feel bored, so that really—
Sewashī hi mo aru shi; busy day *hima na hi mo aru.* leisure day	I have busy days and days of leisure.

§ 127. *Shiu* is a moderately respectful plural particle. It is comparatively little used.

Examples.

Tomodachi shiu.	Friends.
Kodomo shiu.	Children.
Danna shiu.	Masters.

§ 128. *Tachi* or *dachi* is also a respectful plural particle.

Examples.

Ima no fujin dachi ga   When we consider the pursuit
now   lady   (plur.)   of learning by the ladies of the
gakumon wo shite iru no   present time.
learning   doing   remain
wo miru to.
see   if

Mō kimi tachi wa meshi   Have you gentlemen got to the
already   you   rice   rice (the last part of a meal)?
ka?

§ 129. *To.* *To* between two nouns means 'and.' It is sometimes repeated after the second.

Examples.

Watakushi to omaye wa   When you and I came from our
   I   and   you   province.
kuni kara kita toki.
province from came time

Temaye no okubiō to   Putting in the background your
   you   cowardice   cowardice and ignorance.
mugaku to wo tana ni
ignorance   shelf to
agete.
raising

Uchi no inu to dokka no   Our dog and another one have
home   dog   somewhere   killed my aunt's much-prized
inu to ga oba san no daijina   pigeon.
dog   aunt's   much-prized
hato wo koroshita.
pigeon   killed

Note that in the last sentence the whole phrase *uchi no inu to dokka no inu to* is the subject of the sentence and therefore takes *ga* after it as the sign of the nominative case.

Hone to kawa to ni natta.   He has become skin and bone.
bone   skin   has become

Other uses of *to* with nouns.

Shina-jin to kenkwa wo   He had a quarrel with a China-
China man with quarrel   man.
shita.
did

PARTICLES. 145

Kinō   katta   tammono   They are the same as the piece
yesterday bought piece goods   goods I bought yesterday.
to onaji mono desŭ.
as same thing is

Sakujitsu katta   kanakin   They are different from the
yesterday bought   shirtings   shirtings I bought yesterday.
to   chigaimasŭ.
from   differs.

Kono hito   to   issho   Go along with this man.
this man   with same place
ni ike.
go

Are wo tōzoku to   shite   If we look on him as a robber.
him   robber   having made
miru toki wa.
see time

Riōnin   to   mo.   Both of them.
two men and even

Ittō   shokikan to (or *ni*)   He has been made First
first class secretary   Secretary.
narimashĭta.
has become

To with some uninflected words is used to form adverbs.

Shikkari to.	Firmly.
Totsuzen to.	Suddenly.
Pon to.	With a bang.
Bara bara to.	With a rattling noise.

Onomatopoetic words like the two last examples are exceedingly common in Japanese, but they are rather inelegant.

To with nouns sometimes corresponds to the inverted commas used as a sign of quotation.

Urashiwo   to ka iu tokoro.   A place called, if I remember
Vladivostock   ?   right, 'Vladivostock.'

O namaye wa nan' to iu? name what say	What is your name?
Watakŭshi wa Denkichi to I *mōshimas̄.* call	My name is 'Denkichi.'
Hontō to mo (itte yoroshi). truth even saying is good	To be sure it is true.

With verbs, *to* (like our conjunction 'that') is the sign of quotation* or of indirect statement generally, and is used after such verbs as 'to say,' 'to think,' 'to promise,' 'to advise,' etc. etc. It must not be omitted as 'that' often is in English. It must sometimes be rendered by 'to.'

Scri-uri ga mō shimai ni auction already finish *natta to iimashita.* became said	He said that the auction was over.
Ike to iu no da. go (imp.) say is	I tell you to go away.
Nan'da to ye? what is it	What is it you say it is?
Koko de awō to wa here will meet *omowananda.* did not think	I did not expect to meet you here.
Utō to shīta. will strike did	He made to strike him.

When *to* is used, there is often an ellipsis of some part of one of the verbs *iu* 'to say,' *miru* 'to see,' *omou* 'to think,' *suru* 'to do,' *kiku* 'to hear.'

Anata ni sōdan you with consultation *(shō) to (omotte) kimashita.* will do thinking came	I came to consult with you.

---

* I am inclined to think that *to* is identical with the root *so* of *sore* 'that,' and that from a demonstrative, this particle has become a conjunction, just like its English equivalent. In the phrases *to kaku*, *to mo kaku mo*, its original demonstrative force is retained.

PARTICLES.   147

Kōbu   ye   ningaku
engineering   matriculation
(*suru*) *to ka itta.*
   do   ?   said

I think he said he was going to matriculate in Engineering.

Yō   gozarimasŭ   to   (itte)
good   is   that   said
mo (yoroshī).
even   is good

To be sure I will.

Arimasŭ to mo.

To be sure there are.

The ordinary force of *to mo* after verbs is 'though,' 'even though.'

Nani ni   tsukai-harawareru
what for   spend   be paid
to mo omaye no   katte da.
even   your   convenience is

You can spend the money on whatever you please.

In the language of the lower classes, *to* is often contracted with the verbs *iu* and *aru* following.

Ikettara, (for *ike to*
               go (imp.)
ittara)   *ikanai ka?*
when I said not go   ?

Why don't you go when I tell you?

Shiranai   tte (for *to itte*)
not know
iu   ni.
saying in

When I tell you I don't know.

Na   wo   iye   tatte (for
name   say (imp.)
to atte) *sonna hito wa*
 being   such person
arimasenŭ.
is not

You ask me to tell you his name, but there is no such person.

Hongō ye hiki-koshi nasatta
            remove   did
tende   (for *to iu no de*),
by-its-being-said-that
yō-yō no koto de shiremashĭta.
hardly   thing by · found out.

By the help of a statement that you had removed to Hongo, I found you out with difficulty.

Mekura tā (for *to wa*, which   Whom do you call blind?
blind
again is for *to iu wa*) *dare no*
                               who of
koto da?
thing is

Tegami ga nai teba   Have not I told you there is no
letter   is not   letter?
(for *to icba*).
if I say

To after verbs must sometimes be translated 'if' or 'when.'

Gudzu gudzu suru to, tochiu   If you loiter, it will be dark
loitering   do if way   before you get there.
de hi ga kureru yo.
on sun   goes down

Yoku-jitsu ni naru to.   When the following day
next day   become when   arrived.

Sono toki no koto wo   When I think of that time.
that time   thing
omou to.
think

Kuru to sugu ni.   As soon as he comes (or came).
come when at once

§ 130. *Wa* is a distinctive or separative particle. It has the force of isolating or singling out one object from among a number, of opposing one thing to another, or of limiting a statement strictly to the word which *wa* follows. Thus *kore wa* may mean 'this one out of a number,' 'this one not that one,' 'this one and nothing else,' 'this one at least.'

Wa is often found with the subject of a sentence, but it must not be taken for the sign of the nominative case. It is also found combined with the locative particles *ni* and *de*, and even after *wo* the sign of the accusative case, when it takes the *nigori* and becomes *ba*.

The French *quant à* is perhaps the nearest equivalent to *wa*, but in European languages the same idea is usually expressed, not by a separate word, but by means of a greater emphasis on the noun. *Wa* has frequently very little meaning, and its presence or absence is often immaterial. *Wa* may be used after those parts of the verb or adjective which are nouns in syntax.

Shiroi koto wa shiroi. — So far as whiteness *goes*, it is white.

Are wa warui; kore wa yoroshi.
that   is bad   this
is good
— That is bad, this is good.

Kore de wa ikenai.
this with   cannot go
— *This* won't do.

Watakŭshi no kuni ni wa jishin ga nai.
my   country   earthquake   is not
— There are no earthquakes in my country.

Konda wa sonna wake ja (for de wa) nai.
this time   such reason   is not
— *This* time, there will be nothing of that kind.

Dō shitemo san-ya wa kakaru d'arō.
how having done even   three nights   belong will be
— No matter what you do, I think it will take at least three nights.

Hako no uchi ni arimashīta no wa mina motte mairi-mashīta.
box   inside   was   all having taken came
— I brought all that were in the box. (The *wa* implies that there were, or may have been, others not in the box.)

Tōkaidō no ninsoku wa kumosŭke to iu.
coolie   call
— The Tokaido coolies are called *kumosŭke*.

Kono sakana wa takai ka?
this   fish   dear ?
— Is this fish dear?

Hito no mono wa waga mono;
man   thing   my thing
waga mono wa hito no mono
de wa nai.
         is not

What is other people's is mine, but what is mine is not other people's.

Taisa to natte
colonel having become
iru   kara wa.
remain since

Ever since he became a colonel. (The *wa* hints a contrast with the time before he became a colonel.)

Watakŭshi no bunko ni akai
my   desk   red
na-fuda   ichimai aru: sore wo
name card   one   is   that
ba   totte   koi.
  having taken come

There is a red visiting card in my desk: bring it to me. (The *ba* shows that the card is to be singled out among the other things in the desk.)

Saiwai   na koto ni wa.
fortunate   thing in

Fortunately.

Kawagishi no denakatta wa
              not come out
zannen   d'atta.
disappointment was

What a pity Kawagishi was not present!

Narubeku   wa.
become could

If possible.

Kaigun ni irai   shinakŭ
navy   reliance not doing
te wa   naranŭ.
in case does not become

We must rely upon the Navy.

Watakŭshi no sōzō ataru ka
my   idea   hit ?
ataranai ka wa (or *wo*) *shiranŭ.*
not hit

I don't know whether my idea is correct, or not.

Wa without any apparent meaning at the end of a sentence has been already adverted to in § 65. The Kioto terminations *wai na, wa na* suggest that the verb *naru* 'to be' must be supplied in this case, as *mada o kawo ni sŭkoshi mo demasenŭ wa (naru)*, lit. 'not yet coming out in the·least on your face is (a fact),' 'it does not yet show on your face in the least.'

PARTICLES.

An interrogative is often understood after *wa*.

O atsuraye wa (nani de gozarimasŭ)? (hon.) order what is	What do you order, Sir?
Ato wa? next	(What is) the next (course)?
Denkichi san! annaija wa? guide	Mr. Denkichi! what about the guide?
Shikkei nagara, o namaye wa? impolite whilst (hon.) name	Excuse me, but what is your name?

In the common language of Tokio *wa* often suffers change or contraction. Thus for *ari wa shinai ka*, we have *ari ya shinai ka*, for *sore wa*, *sore ya* or *sorya*, for *nanzo wa*, *nanzā*, for *kore wa*, *korā*, for *koto wa*, *kotā*, etc.

§ 131. *Wo* is the sign of the accusative case. But a noun in the accusative case does not necessarily take *wo* after it. The accusative case governed by a preposition does not take *wo*, which is often omitted before *suru* or *itasu* 'to do' and in other cases.

Daiku wa dai wo tsŭkuru. carpenter table makes	The carpenter makes a table.
Ane no yensho to yara wo watakŭshi made kayeshite moraitai. elder sister love letter ? me to return wish to receive	I should like my elder sister's love letter, if that is what you call it, to be returned to me.
Umejirō san no koto bakari wo ki ni kakete iru. thing only mind having hung remain	He thinks of nothing but Umejiro. (Note the position of *wo*.)
Kannin shite kudasare. patience having done give	Please have patience with me. (Note the absence of *wo* after *kannin*.)

| ダヲコ゜ウ テ゛ー, | ヨン ヲ モラウ |

Sazawa wo watakŭshi da to   He thought Sazawa was I.
Sazawa   I
omotta.
thought

Wo is often found where we use a preposition in English.

Iye wo demashĭta.   He left his house.
house from went out

Kuruma wo orite.   Getting out of the jinrikisha.
jinrikisha from having got down

Senyen no kane wo   He was robbed of one thou-
1000 yen   money of   sand yen.
torareta.
was robbed

Konzatsu wo hanareta tokoro.   A place removed from turmoil.
turmoil from removed place

For *mono wo* see *mono*, § 107. In the following sentence *wo* has a somewhat similar meaning:—

Taikō ni mo naru tokoro   It had gone so far that he was
expulsion even become place   on the point of being expelled
de atta wo, dare ka   from college, when by some-
was   whereas somebody   body's good offices—
shiusen shĭte—
good offices having done

But *ga* is commoner than *wo* in this construction.

§ 132. *Ya.* *Ya* oscillates in meaning between the two signs '?' and '!,' being sometimes expressive of doubt, and at others a mere exclamation.

After nouns it is used;—

    1. As a Vocative termination.

      Take ya!   *Take!*

    2. With the meaning 'or.'

Nido ya sando.   Two or three times.
twice   three times

Koto ya samisen wa tai-   A moderate degree of profi-
Jap. harp   guitar   pretty-   ciency on the *koto* or *samisen*
tei de wa ii.   is sufficient.
nearly with   is good

With Verbs.

Kuu ya kuwazu no mi. A person with precarious means
eat or not eat body of subsistence.

Anata no basha wa miyeru The moment your carriage
your carriage is visible comes in sight.
ya inaya.
? not ?

The last idiom is rather bookish.

Ikō ya! Let us go!
will go

For *ya* as a corruption of *wa*, see above, § 130.

§ 133. *Yara.* *Yara* is a contraction for *ya* (see previous section) and *aran*, the old future of *aru*, 'to be.' It expresses uncertainty.

Doko ni orimasŭ yara I don't know where he lives.
where lives ?
watakŭshi ni wa wakarimasenŭ.
me to is not known

Doko ye itta yara. I wonder where he has gone.

The last sentence is left incomplete in the Japanese version. Some such phrase as the concluding words of the previous example is to be supplied.

Amakao to yara ye o ide ni The year after you went to
Macao to went Macao, if that is the right name
narimashĭta yoku nen. of the place.
(respectful) next year

Tanoji tara (for to yara) iu A singing-girl called Tanoji,' if
geisha. I remember rightly.

Dare yara ga itta koto. Something somebody said.
who said thing

§ 134. *Ye,* 'towards,' 'to.' The *y* in this particle is pronounced very lightly, and perhaps the student's safest plan is to omit it altogether, as many Japanese do.

Itsu o kuni ye o kaeri When do you return to your
when country to return country?
nasaru ka?
do ?

Tabi   ye   tatsu   no   wo.   He put off starting on his
journey   starting   journey.
nobashita.
put off

Watakūshi no   yado   ye o   Stay for the night in my
  my   lodging in   lodgings.
tomari nasare.
 stay   do

Achira ye mate.   Wait there.

Ye in the last two sentences seems to mean 'at' or 'in,' but perhaps *o ide nasatte* or *itte* is to be supplied after it.

There is a *ye* (or *e*) which is a mere interjection something like our 'eh?,' and must be distinguished from *ye* 'towards.'

§ 135. *Yo.* *Yo* is used with nouns in the vocative case, but it is something more than a mere vocative particle. It is emphatic, and implies pleading, remonstrance, appeal or warning. Indeed it often stands quite by itself as an exclamation with this force. It is difficult to render *yo* by any English word, but 'I tell you,' will sometimes translate it pretty accurately. In the Kioto dialect *yo* is used with the roots of verbs of the second conjugation to form the imperative mood. Thus for *tabero*, the Kioto people say *tabeyo*. In the Tokio dialect, *yo* with the imperative is not a mere termination, but has the emphatic force described above. It is a favourite particle with women.

Okka   san yo.   Mother!
 mother

O cha yo! o   yukata   yo!   Some tea! a bath gown! (for
  tea   bath gown   a guest).

Abunai   yo.   It is dangerous, I tell you.
is dangerous

Shiranai yo.   I tell you I don't know.

O ide yo.	Do come.
O agari nasai (for *nasare*) *yo.* come up do	Do come in.

§ 136. *Yori*, 'from,' 'since,' 'than.'

Examples.

Kore yori hachi ri. this from eight	Eight ri from here.
Konaida yori biōki some days ago from illness *de shukkin* owing to going to office *itashimasenŭ.* do not	For some days past I have been prevented by illness from going to office.
Mōshi-agemashĭta nedan yori stated price than *shĭta de wa sashi-agerarare-* low with offer can *masenŭ.* not	I can't let you have them for less than I said.
Omotta yori yasui. thought cheap	It is cheaper than I thought.
Watakŭshi yori hoka ni me than other *shiru hĭto wa nashi.* know man is not	Nobody knows but me.
Itsumo yori kenkō desŭ. ever than robust is	He is in stronger health than usual.
Seppuku suru yori hoka ni harakiri do than other *shikata ga nai.* do-side is not	There is nothing left for it but to commit harakiri.
A. *Ō! Fuku ka? dō* Hilloa! how *shĭta?* B. *Ore yori wa omaye* did me than you *san dō shĭta?* how did	A. Hilloa! is that Fuku? What became of you? B. Or rather what became of you?

§ 137. *Zo* is a very emphatic particle.

Examples.

Keshite   uchi ye   irete   You must positively not allow
positively   house into admit   him into the house.

  wa   naranai   zo.
in case   not become

Kataku   ii-tsŭketa zo.   You have my strict orders.
hard   ordered

Kita   zo.   Here he is!
has come

Kiku   hodo   no mono wa   I tell you there is nothing
hear   quantity   thing   worth listening to.

nai ze (for *zo ye*).
is not

CHAPTER X.

ADVERBS, PREPOSITIONS, CONJUNCTIONS AND INTERJECTIONS.

ADVERBS.

§ 138. The true adverb is in Japanese the form of the adjective ending in the syllable *ku;* as *hayaku,* 'quickly;' *atarashiku,* 'newly;' *yoku,* 'well.'* See § 82. Many words used as adverbs are really nouns or nouns followed by particles, as *ashita,* 'tomorrow;' *sakini,* 'before;' *bakani,* 'foolishly;' *suguni,* 'at once;' or participles of verbs, as *subete,* 'generally;' *semete,* 'at least;' *nokorazu,* 'without exception.'

The present indicative of verbs is sometimes reduplicated to form an adverb, as *miru-miru,* 'à vue d'oeil', *yuku-yuku,* 'as one goes along.'

§ 139. The following list contains some of the most commonly used adverbs :—

ADVERBS OF TIME.

Mō, already.
Itsu, when (interrogative).
Toki, ditto. (relative).
Miōnichi, to-morrow.
Ashita, ditto.
Konnichi, to-day.
Kiō, ditto.

Mada, not yet.
Itsudemo, always.
Jikini, soon.
Mettani, (with neg.) seldom.
Tadaima, immediately.
Mōhaya, already.
Sudeni, ditto.

* Also contracted into *hayō, atarashiu, yō.*

ADVERBS.

ADVERBS OF TIME.

Sakujitsŭ, yesterday.
Kinō, ditto.
Sendatte, some days ago.
Nochihodo, by and by.

Tabi tabi, several times.
Ichi do or *hĭto tabi*, once.
Ni do or *fŭta tabi*, twice.
&c. &c.

ADVERBS OF PLACE.*

Koko, here.
Kokoni, here.
Doko, where.
Dokoni, where.
Soko, there.
Sokoni, there.
Asŭko, there.
Asŭkoni, there.
Kochi, here, hither.
Kochira, here, hither.
Dochi, where, whither.

Dochira, where, whither.
Sochi, there, thither.
Sochira, there, thither.
Achi, there, thither.
Achira, there, thither.
Sakini, before.
Atode, behind.
Sakasama, upside down.
Yokoni, across.
Uyeni, above.
Shĭtani, below.

ADVERBS OF MANNER.

Dō, how.
Ikaga, how.
Kō, in this way.
Kayōni, in this way.
Sō, in that way.
Sayōni, in that way.

Dōmo, howsoever.
Hanahada, very.
Naze, why.
Zehi, positively.
Jōzu ni, cleverly.
Yoku, well.

ADVERBS OF QUANTITY.

Takŭsan, *taisō*, much.
Donokurai, how much.
Jiubun, enough.
Sŭkoshi, little.
Ikutsŭ, how many.

Bakari, only.
Ikura, how much.
Motto, more.
Amari or } too much.
Yokeini }

---

* See also §§ 18 to 24.

ADVERBS OF AFFIRMATION AND NEGATION.

He, or *hai*, yes.
Iye, no.
Mottomo, right!

He or *hai* must not be understood in too strict a sense. It is often nothing more than a polite expression of attention to what is being said. The true mode of expressing affirmation is to repeat the verb of the clause referred to.

A negative answer to a question may be expressed in a similar manner. *He* and *hai* are more used in answer to commands than to questions.

Examples.

Mō kimashīta ka?	Has he come yet?
Kimashīta.	Yes, he has come.
Miōnichi tsugō wa tomorrow convenience	Is it convenient tomorrow?
yoroshī ka? is good	
Sayō desŭ or *He, sayō desŭ.*	Yes, it is.
He, sayō de gozaimasenū.	No, it is not.

§ 140. Onomatopoetic Adverbs are common in Japanese but most of them are somewhat vulgar. They are often followed by the particle *to*.

Examples.

Gata gata.	of a rattling noise.
Butsu butsu.	grumblingly.
Potsuri-potsuri.	of the 'spitting' of rain.
Domburi to.	of falling with a 'flop.'

The adverb invariably precedes the word which it qualifies.

PREPOSITIONS.

§ 141. The Preposition should in Japanese be called the Postposition, as it always follows the noun. The prepositions have been treated of in the Chapter on Particles.

The English prepositions must often be rendered in Japanese by different parts of speech. Thus, for 'between,' we have *no aida ni*, lit. 'in the space of;' for 'beside' we must say *no soba ni*, lit. 'at the side of;' for 'over,' *koyete*, the past participle of *koyeru*, 'to cross.'

CONJUNCTIONS.

§ 142. Conjunctions in English are variously rendered in Japanese by Particles, Verbal or Adjectival terminations etc. Some have been already noticed under the head of Particles, and hints as to translating them into Japanese will also be found in Chapter XI.

INTERJECTIONS.

§ 143. As in other languages Interjections are merely exclamations, and can scarcely be said to have any grammar. The principal are :—

Oi, Halloa!
Aita, Ah! of pain.
Oya, Oh! of surprise—used chiefly by women.
He, (rising accent) of surprise and admiration.
Yai, of terror.
Dokkoi, when lifting a heavy weight, or otherwise exerting oneself.
Sā, of inciting a person to do something.
Mā, of satisfaction, surprise, etc.

The *ne* so common in the vulgar Yedo dialect (in other parts of Japan it is *na* or *nō*) is a sort of interjection. It has very little meaning, and merely serves to draw the attention of the person addressed. It has about the same force as the meaningless, 'you know,' sometimes heard in English conversation. *Yoroshi ne*, 'it is good, is it not'? *mata miōnichi o ide nasaru ne*, 'you will come again to-morrow, won't you'? *sore kara ne*——, 'after that, don't you know——'

Ne is little used by men.

CHAPTER XI.

ENGLISH WORDS INTO JAPANESE.

§ 144. At the risk of some repetition, it has been considered desirable to give a few notes on the mode of rendering into Japanese some common English words.*

§ 145. 'Although' or 'though.' *Keredo* with indicatives or verbal forms of adjectives, as *itta keredo* 'although he went,' *samui keredo* 'although it is cold'; participle and *mo* or adverb and *te mo*, as *itte mo* 'although having gone,' *samukŭ te mo* 'though cold'; concessive form, as *ikedomo* 'although (he) go,' *samukeredo*, 'although cold.'

§ 146. 'And.' Connecting nouns, *to*, which is often repeated after the last noun, as *sake to sakana*, 'wine and fish;' *kore to are to*, 'this and that:' *ni*, as *kashi ni kudamono* 'cakes and fruit.' Sometimes the nouns are simply placed together as *sake sakana* 'wine and fish.' See also *dano*, § 111 and *no*, § 122. Connecting verbs, 'and' is expressed by putting the first verb in the participle form, at least where the action of the first verb is conceived as preparatory or preliminary to that of the one succeeding it, as *tokkuri wo akete motte koi*, 'open the bottle and bring it here.' In other cases, and at the beginning of a sentence, *soshite* or *sore ni* is used for 'and.' When Adjectives are joined by 'and,' the first is usually put in the adverbial form followed by *te*, as *yasukŭte atatakai* 'it is cheap and warm. See also *shi*, § 126, and *de*, § 111.

* The subject of this chapter has been more fully dealt with in Dr. Imbrie's excellent 'Japanese Etymology.' Messrs. Satow and Ishibashi's Dictionary should also be consulted.

§ 147. 'As.' 'As you know,' *go zonji no tōri*, lit. 'the manner of your knowing'; 'as you say,' *ossharu tōri;* 'as dear as that,' *sore hodo takai;* 'as many as possible,' *narutake* or *ṇarubeku takŭsan;* 'as soon as finished,' *dekishidai* or *deki-agaru to sugu ni;* 'as far as,' *made;* 'as it is,' *sono mama;* 'as I was going out,' *deru toki;* 'just as I was going out,' *deru tokoro de;* 'the same as mine,' *watakushi no to onaji koto.*

§ 148. 'Because.' *Kara, yuye, yuye ni,* all of which are used after verbs in the indicative mood and adjectives in the verbal form: 'because why,' *naze nareba;* 'Oh! just because,' *naze demo.*

§ 149. 'Before' is usually *no maye ni,* as *me no maye ni,* 'before one's eyes;' *Nichi-yō no maye ni,* 'before Sunday;' *maye ni kiita,* 'I heard before;' *deru maye ni,* 'before he goes (or went) out.' 'Before he comes' may be rendered *kimasenŭ uchi ni* or *kuru maye ni.*

§ 150. 'But.' Instead of a conjunction like our 'but,' the constructions with *mo* or the concessive forms described in § 145 are preferred. See also under *ga,* § 123.

At the beginning of a sentence, 'but' may be rendered by *shikashi, shikashi nagara, datte, daga,* or *demo.* 'There is but one,' *hitotsu shika nai.*

§ 151. 'Can,' 'could.' 'I can go,' *iku koto ga dekiru, ikareru;* 'you can go,' (permission), *ittemo yoroshi;* 'can't you come?,' *o ide nasaru wake ni wa mairimasenŭ ka?;* 'I could not come,' *kuru koto wa dekimasenanda, koraremasenŭ d'atta.*

§ 152. 'If.' 'If' is usually expressed by one of the Conditional or Hypothetical terminations of Verbs, the participle and *wa,* or the indicative with *toki wa* or *to.*

To for 'if' is often preceded by a present tense where we should expect a past, as *atarashi no desŭ to ikenai kara kareta no motte kimashĭta,* 'as it would not have done if it had been a new one, I brought a seasoned one.' 'Even if' is expressed by the participle and *mo,* in which case the verb is sometimes preceded by *tatoye,* 'supposing that.' *Moshi* is sometimes prefixed to the verb when a mere hypothesis is intended. *Man-ichi,* 'one in ten thousand,' followed by the indicative with *toki wa,* may be used when a bare possibility is spoken of.

§ 153. 'May,' 'might.' 'You may go,' (permission) *itte mo yoroshi*; 'there may be some,' *aru ka mo shirenŭ*; 'so that all may hear,' *mina ni kikoyeru yōni;* 'I think I may perhaps go,' *ikō ka to omou*; 'I said you might go,' *itte mo yoroshi to itta;* 'you might have warmed my clothes,' *kimono de mo attamete okeba yoi ni.*

§ 154. 'Must.' 'I must go,' *ikaneba naranŭ, ikanakŭte wa naranŭ, ikanai to narimasenŭ;* 'you must have noticed that pretty woman,' *ano bijin wa me ni tsukanŭ hadzu wa nai;* 'you must be aware,' *go shōchi no nai hadzu wa nai;* 'you must have been bored' *sazo go taikutsu de'mashitarō.* See also §§ 59, 94, 95.

§ 155. 'Or.' *Ya* between two nouns; *ka* repeated with both alternatives. See §§ 132 and 115. 'Or' is sometimes not expressed, as *go roku nen,* five or six years; *go shinzō omaye nomitakereba,* 'if your wife or you wants to drink.'

§ 156. 'Ought.' 'You ought not to do that,' *sō shĭte wa sumanai;* 'what ought I to do?' *dō itashĭtara yokarō?* 'I ought to have told you my name,' *namaye mōshi-agereba yoroshiu gozarimashĭta.* See also §§ 95 (*beki*) and 105 (*hadzu*).

§ 157. 'Should.' 'If any one should come,' *moshi mo hito ga kitara ;* "if you had not fired, I should have been killed,' *anata wa teppō wo utanakereba, watakŭshi wa inochi wọ torarete shimau no da ;* 'you should go at once,' *sugu ni o ide nasaru ga yokarō ;* 'if that should happen,' *moshi sō iu koto ga atta toki ni wa ;* 'if I had time, I should go,' *hima ga attara, ikō ga.* See also 'ought' and 'must.'

§ 158. 'That.' 'That' as a conjunction is usually *to* (see § 129). ' Please tell (your master) that it is somebody who has a trifling request to make of him,' *sŭkoshi go irai no suji ga atte maitta mono da to kō itte kure.* Other modes of rendering 'that;' 'I am sorry that I did not do so sooner,' *hayaku shi-nakatta ga zannen da*; 'take care that it does not catch fire,' *hi ga kakaranai yō ni yōjin shiro.* For 'that' as a relative and as a demonstrative pronoun see §§ 20, 21 and 28.

§ 159. 'Think' is in Japanese *omou.* 'I think of going,' *ikō to omou, ikō ka to omou.* Other ways of translating think : 'what do you think of doing,' *ikaga nasaru tsumori desŭ ;* 'I think he has come,' *mō kimashĭta to omotte imasŭ, mō kimashĭtarō* ; 'I think he will go,' *ikimasŭ deshō ;* 'I don't think it is ready,' *mada shĭtaku wa dekimasŭ mai.*

§ 160. 'To.' For 'to' as a preposition with nouns see *ni, ye* and *made,* Ch. IX., §§ 121, 134 and 118.

Where it is used with verbs to form an infinitive mood 'to' must be variously translated according to circumstances, as ' I am unable to go,' *iku koto ga dekinai ;* 'I want to go,' *ikitai ;* 'I have to go,' *ikaneba naranŭ ;* 'it is too late to go,' *mō iku ni wa osoi ;* 'do you intend to go?' *iku tsumori ka ;* 'tell him to go,' *ike to itte o kure :* 'tell him to send me some money,' *kane wo okuru yō ni hanashĭte kure;* 'it is easy to go,' *iku koto wa yasui;* 'he promised to come,' *kuru to yakŭsoku shĭta;* 'it is arranged that he is to go,' *iku koto ni kimatta;* 'he has gone to buy,' *kai ni itta;* 'it won't do to be late,' *osokŭ te wa ikenai.*

§ 161. 'Want.' 'I want money,' *kane ga iru*; 'I want to go,' *ikitai*; 'I don't want to go,' *ikitaku nai*; 'do you want this?' *kore wa o iryō desŭ ka?, kore wa hoshī ka?;* 'I want to buy,' *kai ni kimashĭta.*

§ 162. 'Would.' 'He said he would go,' *iku* (or *ikō*) *to itta;* 'I thought you would be here,' *koko ni o ide nasaru d'arō to omotta;* 'I would have come today but—' *konnichi kuru no deshĭta ga—;* 'if he came, what would you do,' *kitara dō nasaru;* 'it would have been better if he had gone,' *itta hō ga yok'atta, ittara yok'atta.*

'I would get some tea ready, only the fire has gone out,' *cha wo irerunda (ireru no da) ga, hi ga kiyete shimatta;* 'if my father had been alive, I am sure he would have been pleased,' *ottotsusan go zonjō nara, o yorokobi nasaimashō.*

CHAPTER XII.

HONORIFIC AND HUMBLE FORMS.

§ 163. One of the chief difficulties which confront the foreigner whose ambition it is to speak Japanese with accuracy and propriety is the use of the honorific and humble forms of expression. Grammatical rules, however, go but a short way in teaching their use, and much must be left to the student's experience and observation.

It may be taken that the honorific forms are chiefly appropriated to verbs, nouns, and pronouns in the second person, though they are also used in speaking respectfully of absent persons. The humble forms belong to the first person, and the polite termination *masŭ* is used indiscriminately with all three persons.

It will be seen below that there is a considerable variety of honorific and humble expressions, varying according to the rank of the person addressed. But even in speaking to the same person, forms, the neglect of which on a first introduction or on other formal occasions would be a gross breach of decorum, may be dropped without offence in the heat of an argument, or in the freedom of more familiar intercourse. Women use honorifics more than men, and they are less frequent in dependent than in principal clauses.

§ 164. Respect and humility are indicated in the following ways :—

HONORIFIC AND HUMBLE FORMS. 167

1. By special honorific or humble nouns, pronouns or verbs.*
2. By honorific prefixes.
3. By honorific suffixes.

§ 165. Honorific and humble nouns.

Examples.

Neutral.	Humble.	Honorific.
Ko or *kodomo*, child.	*Segare* (my son).	*(Go) shisoku* (your son).
Kanai, wife.	——	*Saikun* (your wife).
Iye, house.	——	*(O) taku* (your house).

Chinese words are commonly considered more elegant than their Japanese synonymes, and are therefore sometimes preferred in polite speech. Thus for *o sake, go shiu* is considered a more polite term; *go ran nasare* 'look' is preferred to *o mi nasare* and *go zonji de gozarimasŭ*, 'you know,' is always said instead of *o shiri nasaru*.

It is chiefly in speaking of the relations of one's self and of others, more particularly of the person addressed, that humble and honorific words are used. Special humble nouns are, however, not very numerous, the absence of honorific forms being usually considered sufficient. The following list of relations which has been taken, with some alterations, from Mr. Satow's 'Kuaiwa Hen' will serve as a guide to the use of these words. With some, the honorific prefixes described in § 167 are used, or the suffixes mentioned in § 168.

RELATIONS.

Another's wife.	One's own wife.
o kami san { all under the rank of *samurai*.	*niōbō*.

---

* The honorific and humble distinctions of pronouns have been already noticed in Chapter IV.

go kanai	lower rank	*sai.*
saikun	of official.	*kanai.*
oku san	gentlemen	
oku sama	of	*kanai.*
go naishitsu	rank.	

Old-fashioned people sometimes say *gusai* ('stupid wife') for their own wives.

Another's husband.
  danna.
  teishi (familiar).
  go teishi.

One's own husband.
  tsure-ai (by the lower class).
  danna or *teishi.*
  yado.

But in general the husband's surname is used both in addressing the wife and by her in speaking of her husband, in the former case with *san* added, in the latter without *san*

Another's father.
  go sompu.
  ototsu san (to children).

One's own father.
  oyaji.
  chichi.

Another's mother.
  go bokō.
  haha sama.
  okka san (to children).
  go rōbo (when aged).

One's own mother.
  haha.
  o fukuro.
  okka (by children).

Another's grandfather.
  go sofu sama.
  go sofu.
  o ji sama } to children.
  o ji san

One's own grandfather.
  sofu.
  jiji.

Another's grandmother.
  go sobo.
  o bā san (to children).

One's own grandmother.
  sobo.
  baba.

Another's brother.
  o ani san (elder).
  go sonkei (do).
  go shatei sama (younger).
  go shatei (do).
  otōto go (do).

One's own brother.
  ani.
  otōto.

HONORIFIC AND HUMBLE FORMS. 169

Another's sister.
o *ane san* (elder).
ane san.
o *imōto go* (younger).

One's own sister.
ane.
imōto.

Another's son.
go shisoku.
o *musŭko san.*

One's own son.
segare.
musŭko.
kodomo (also of daughters).

go sōriō (eldest).
go jinan (second).
go sannan (third).

sōriō.
jinan.
sannan.

Another's daughter.
go sokujo.
o *musŭme go.*
o *jō san.*

One's own daughter.
musŭme.

Oji and *oba* are used for one's own uncle and aunt; the same words followed by *san* or *sama* for another's.

Oi and *mei* are used for one's own nephew and niece; *oi go sama* and *o mei go sama* for another's.

Another's father-in-law and mother-in-law are *shiuto go, shiutome go;* one's own simply *shiuto, shiutome.*

Similarly one's own son-in-law is *muko*, another's *o muko san;* daughter-in-law (own) *yome* or (another's) *o yome go ;* grandchild (own) *mago* or (another's) *o mago ;* cousin (own) *itoko* or (another's) *o itoko ;* adopted son, (own) *yōshi* or (another's) *go yōshi.* *San* or *sama* may be added to any of the above honorific forms.

Children, and to some extent women, add *san* in speaking of their own elder relations. They say, for instance, *ane san* for 'my elder sister,' *okka san* for 'my mamma.'

The words used of one's own relations may also be used of the relations of third persons to whom no special respect is due, or even of the relatives of the person addressed when the latter is of a rank decidedly inferior to the speaker.

To one's servant, one says *omaye no chichi* or *omaye no oyaji* for 'your father.'

Segare and *gusai* can only be used of one's own son, and one's own wife.

§ 166. Honorific and humble verbs. Honorific verbs are of two kinds (a) where a wholly different word is substituted for the ordinary verb and (b) where the causative or potential (passive) verb is put instead of the simple verb, on the principle that it is more respectful to say that a person has caused a thing to be done or has been able to do it than merely that he has done it. Humble verbs belong exclusively to the first of these two classes.

Examples.

(a)

Neutral.	Humble.	Honorific.
Suru, to do	*Itasu* or *tsukamatsuru*	*Nasaru* or *asobasu*.
Iku, to go	*Mairu*	*O ide nasaru* or *irassharu*.
Iu, to say	*Mōsu*	*Ossharu*.
Yaru, to give	*Ageru*	*Kudasaru* or *tamau*.
Taberu, to eat	——	*Meshi-agaru*.
Omou, to think	——	*Oboshimesu*.

(b)

Doitsu no Kōtei ga Germany Emperor *shinaremashita,* was able to die.	The German Emperor is dead.
Daijin ga deraremashita. H. E.	His Excellency (used of Ministers of State) has gone out.
Himei ni without command (i.e. of *shinaremashita.* Heaven) died.	He died a violent death.
O machi asobase.	Be pleased to wait.

§ 167. Honorific Prefixes. The honorific prefixes *o* and *go* are used before nouns, verbs and adjectives, as indications of respect. They generally, though not invariably, show that the words with which they are used are in the second person or have something to do with the person addressed, and they therefore render to a large extent unnecessary the use of pronouns of the second person. Thus *o mŭma*, *o kuruma* will usually mean 'your horse,' 'your jinrikisha' without the addition of any personal pronoun. Sometimes however the pronoun understood is not in the possessive but in some other case. *O negai*, for example, usually means 'a petition *to* you' and *o mŭma* may only mean 'a horse *for* you,' as in the phrase *osore-itta o mŭma de gozarimasŭ*, 'it is a fear-entered honourable horse' i.e. 'it is a horse I am ashamed to offer you.' The phrase *o saki ye* means 'before you.' It is an apology for going on ahead of or leaving before the person addressed. *Go henji* (honorable answer) may mean according to circumstances, either 'your answer' or 'an answer to you'; *go burei* either 'your impoliteness' or 'impoliteness to you.'

Sometimes the honorifics are intended by way of respect to the objects to which they are applied. There are words with which the lower classes use them almost invariably, partly from this reason, and partly no doubt from habit. 'The sun' for example is *o tentō sama* with women of the lower class, 'cold water' is *o hiya*, 'hot water' *o yu*, 'food' *go zen*, 'cash' *o ashi*, 'a Buddhist temple' *o tera* etc. etc.

O is a word of Japanese origin, no doubt connected with *ōki*, 'great,' and is ordinarily prefixed to Japanese words. *Go* is used before Chinese words. But neither of these rules is without exceptions. A good number of Chinese words have become so assimilated that their Chinese origin is overlooked, and they are no longer recognized as strangers. They therefore take the native prefix, while on the other hand one or two Japanese words have come to be sometimes preceded by *go*. Ex. *O taku*, 'your house;' *o kyaku*, 'a guest;' *o tokei*, 'your watch;' *go mottomo*, 'you are right;' *go* (or *o*) *yururi to*, 'at your ease' (in pressing a guest to stay longer).

A very common use of *o* is with the stems of verbs in the second person followed by the honorific verbs *nasaru* or *asobasu* as *o kashi nasare* 'lend,' *o kashi nasatte kudasare*, 'please be kind enough to lend me,' *o machi asobase*, 'be good enough to wait, sir.'

This combination is very common in the imperative mood when *nasare* is sometimes contracted into *na* or even omitted altogether. But in such cases the honorific force almost entirely disappears. *O machi na* or *o machi* 'wait' would only be used to servants or members of one's own family.

O is also used before the stem followed by the humble word *mōsu* in the first person, so that this construction comprises an expression of respect for the person addressed with a humble reference to oneself. Ex. *O negai mōshimasŭ* 'I ask a favor of you, *o tanomi mōsu** 'I pray you.'

O may also be used with adjectives. Ex. *O samuu gozarimashō* 'I am sure you are cold,' *o wakō gozarimasŭ* 'you are young.'

In the compound *gozarimasŭ* or *gozaimasŭ*, so common as a polite substitute for the verb *aru* 'to be,' *go* is not a honorific particle indicative of respect to the person who is the subject of the verb, but like *masŭ*, its use implies

---

* This phrase or *o tanomu, tanomu* or *o tanomi moshimasŭ* is called out by the visitor to a Japanese house instead of knocking or ringing a bell.

HONORIFIC AND HUMBLE FORMS. 173

courtesy to the person addressed whatever may be the nominative to it. When we say *watakŭshi de gozaimasŭ* 'it is I,' *are de gozaimasŭ* 'it is he,' there is no intention of speaking honorifically of oneself or of him; the courtesy implied by the use of *go* is all intended for the benefit of the person addressed.

§ 168. HONORIFIC SUFFIXES.

The Plural Suffixes *gata* and *tachi* and in a less degree *shiu* have a moderately honorific force: *ra* and *domo* are used when no honorific meaning is intended.

Sama, the original meaning of which is 'appearance,' is used after the name, description or title in addressing or in speaking respectfully of superiors, more especially by servants to their masters, and by tradespeople to their customers. It indicates much the same degree of respect as our 'Sir.' Ex. *Danna sama* 'Sir,' *anata sama* 'your honour,' *Takeda sama* Mr. Takeda, *oku sama* 'the honourable interior of the house,' i.e. 'the lady of the house,' *kōshi sama* 'the Minister,' *Tenshi sama* 'the Mikado,' *o Tentō sama* 'the sun,' *tono sama* (to daimios) 'your Lordship.' It is also used with a few other words, as *go kurō sama* 'thanks for your trouble,' *o sewa sama* 'I am much obliged to you.' *Kochira sama*, *achira sama* are highly respectful expressions for *kochira*, *achira*.

San, a contraction of *sama*, corresponds roughly to our Mr., Mrs. or Miss. It is used chiefly between equals, occasionally to superiors and even to inferiors when one wishes to be civil. It is not used with reference to one's own relations or in addressing one's own servants. 'My father' is not *oyaji san* but simply *oyaji*. *San* may be added either to the personal name or to the surname. In the case of women *o* is usually prefixed at the same time, when the personal name is used, as *O Tora san* 'Miss Tora.' To one's own servant or wife the personal name with or without *o* is used. A wife does not speak of or call her husband——*san;* a concubine does. In speaking of her husband in the third person, a wife generally says *yado* 'the house' or *teishiu* (pron. *teishi*), 'husband.' *San* is not used to one's friend's servants. But to the servants of strangers *don* should be used instead of *san*. 'Madame' is *oku san* or in a lower class of society *o kami san*. 'Mademoiselle' is *o jō san* or *o musume go*. In the third person for Mrs. A——, A—— *san no go kanai* or *saikun* is the proper expression. *San* is much used after names of trades and professions, as *daiku san* 'the carpenter,' *bantō san* 'the merchant's clerk,' *isha san* 'the doctor,' both in the second and in the third person.

Children use to each other the first part of the personal name with or without *san*. One's own male servants are addressed by their personal names which are mostly abbreviated, as *Tsune* for *Tsunesaburō*. Little boys up to five or six are called *bō chan* (for *bō san*).

Dono is little used in speaking but its contraction *don* is used in addressing or in speaking of the servants of others, also by female servants and *bantos* (merchant's clerks) to each other.

Kun is the word in use by students for Mr.. It is familiar, like the use of the bare surname in English. The surname without any addition is an exceedingly familiar form of address, and is little used.

As an example of the use of these suffixes, take your servant. His full name is *Ikeda Torakichi*, *Ikeda* being the surname and *Torakichi* the personal name. You will address him as *Tora* or *Torakichi*; his intimates of his own rank will call him *Tora san* or perhaps *Ikeda san;* his wife *Ikeda*, and strangers *Ikeda san;* if his son goes to the university or is drawn as a conscript, he will be called by his comrades *Ikeda kun*, and if he becomes an official his subordinates will address him and speak of him as *Ikeda sama*.

On visiting cards, the personal name, surname and title or official rank only are written. No *san* or other similar suffix is used.

Go is used as a suffix after a few names of relationships. See the Table in § 166.

§ 169. The above modes of expressing respect or humility are generally found in combination. Thus the phrase *o ide nasaremase* includes the honorific particle *o*, the special verbs *ideru* instead of *iku* or *kuru*, and *nasaru* for *suru*, and the potential form *nasareru* for *nasaru*.

Masu was originally a honorific. As now used, it expresses neither respect nor humility but is a polite termination which may be used indiscriminately with any person of the verb. It should be remembered that *masŭ* is an element of the contracted forms *desŭ, deshita* and *deshō*, which are therefore somewhat more polite than *da, datta,* and *darō*. But a contracted form which contains a honorific or polite form is always much less respectful than the uncontracted form. The politeness implied in the use of *masŭ* is always for the benefit of the person addressed, and not of third persons.

It should not be used to servants or coolies.

§ 170. Examples of Honorific and Humble expressions. See also the extracts in Chapter XVI.

Nouns.

A. Go shiu (for sake) wa ikaga de gozarimasŭ? B. Hai, chūdai itashimashō.
how   is
receive   will do

A. May I offer you some sake? B. Thanks, I will take some.

O tsumuri (for atama) kara saki ni itashimashō ka?
head   from first
shall do   ?

Shall I do your head first, Sir? (a shampooer asks).

✓ Go zen (for meshi) ga dekimashĭta.
meal

Dinner (breakfast or supper) is ready, Sir.

Go zen tsubu de tsukete o kure.
boiled rice grains having
stuck   give

Stick it on with some boiled rice.

A. Yū go han wa mada de gozaimasŭ ka? B. He; yū-meshi wa mada desŭ.

A. Have you not had supper yet? B. No, not yet.

Verbs.

✓ O machi mōshite (humble for shĭte) orimashĭta.
wait doing
remained

I was waiting for you.

Kataku go chiukoku mōshimasŭ (humble for suru).
hard   advice   do

I strongly advise you.

Go konrei asobasanai (honorif. for suru) uchi.
marriage do not
within

Before you perform the marriage.

O suki asobasu ongaku.
like do   music

The music which your Lordship is so fond of.

Oki-tamaye.
put give

Have done. (student's language).

O rei wo o uke mōsu hodo no koto de wa gozaimasenŭ.
thanks receive do amount
thing   is not

It is not worth being thanked for.

O hima no toki o hanashi / When you have time, please
leisure   time   talk   come and have a chat.
ni irasshatte (for kite) kudasare.
having come   give

Donata de irasshaimasŭ ka?   May I ask who you are, Sir?
who   are (for aru)

Nan'to osshaimashita?   What did you say, Sir?
what   say (for itta)

Miōnichi o kayeshi mōshimasŭ.   I will return it tomorrow.
tomorrow   return   do

Haiken shitemo   May I see it?
see having done even
(for mitemo) ii no desŭ ka?
           good   is it

Haishaku shite wa   Would it be any harm if I
borrow having done   borrowed it?
warui ka?
bad

Honorific Prefixes.

O toshi wa o ikutsu ni o   What age are you?
   year   how many
nari nasaru?
become do

O toshi ni shite wa o tassha   You are a robust man for your
   year   robust   age.
de gozarimasŭ.
is

O medetō gozarimasŭ.   I beg to compliment you. (a new
beautiful   year's greeting, also used at wed-
                      dings etc.)

O yakamashiu gozarimashita.   I have been making myself a
noisy   nuisance to you.

Makoto ni o sewa da.   I am much obliged to you (said
truly   trouble   ironically or to inferiors).

O atsuu gozarimasŭ.   It is hot.
hot

O shidzuka ni irasshaimase.   Go in peace. (to a departing
quietly   be, go or come.   guest).

Danna wa o uchi ka?   Is your master at home?
master   within

Oku sama wa o uchi ka?	Is your mistress at home?
He, o rusu de gozarimasŭ. absent	No, he (or she) has gone out.
O dekake de gozarimasŭ.	Ditto.
O urami ni wa zonjimasenŭ. hate not think	I don't hate you for it.
Anata wa o wakai kara. you are young because	Because you are young.
Anata no o kangaye de wa. opinion with	In your opinion.
O kage de. shadow with	Thanks to you.
O jama wo itashimashĭta. interference did	I apologize for having interrupted you.
Doko ni o sumai desŭ ka? where dwell is	Where do you (or your father, master etc.) live?
Otoko no o ko desŭ ka; onna male child is female *no o ko desŭ ka?* child	Is it (your friend's child) a boy or a girl?
Danna! o mukai ni mairi- master meet have *mashĭta.* come	I have come to meet you, Sir.
O machi nasare.	Wait.
Koko ni kite o kure here having come give (*nasare*).	Come here.
O aki ni nattara wata- empty when became *kŭshi ni kashĭte kurenu ka?* me having lent give not	Won't you lend it to me when you have done with it?
O tsuki sama ni suppon da. moon tortoise	It is as different as chalk from cheese.
Yoku o tadzune kudasatta. well visit have given	Thank you for coming to see me.
O kinodoku sama. mind of poison	I am sorry for you.
O machidō deshĭta.	I have kept you waiting.

HONORIFIC AND HUMBLE FORMS.   179

Go mendō de gozaimashō trouble will be ga—	It will be troubling you very much, but—
Go shimpai ni wa oyobi- anxiety reaches masenŭ. not	You need not be anxious.
Go katte shidai. convenience according to	Just as you please.
Goran nasai!	Look!
Gomen nasai!	Pardon me!: I beg your pardon.
Gyoi (for go i) ni gozaimasŭ. hon. opinion is	Your Honour is quite right.
Mada go menkai mōshimasenŭ yet meeting do not deshita. was	I have not met you before.
Go yenrio naku—	Without ceremony.
Sazo go shiushō de surely sorrow gozaimashō. will be	You must surely be in great grief (a common expression of condolence).
Iro iro go yakkai ni all kinds of assistance narimashita. become	I am under all kinds of obligations to you.
Goran no tōri. see manner	As you see.
Tōke no go shisoku this house son Hayazō kun. Mr.	Your son Hayazō.
Go isshin maye. restoration before	Before the Restoration (of the Mikado's power in 1868).

Suffixes.

O kyaku sama ga miyema- visitor has be- shita. come visible	A visitor has arrived, Sir.

A. *Uyeki-ya san!* *kono ki*　　A. Gardener! is not this tree
　　gardener　　　this tree　　dying? B. Yes. Sir; I'll trans-
wa kareru ja nai ka? B.　　plant it over there.
　wither
He! achira sama ye
　　there　　　　to
uye-kayemashō.
plant change.

Danna sama ni mōshi-wake　　My conduct has been inexcus-
　master　　　　　excuse　　　able, Sir.
ga gozarimasenŭ.

Yome go san no go biōki　　How is your daughter-in-law?
　daughter-in-law　　illness
wa ikaga de gozaimasŭ?
　how

Kono fujin gata wo　　Show these ladies to the waiting
　　ladies　　　　　　　room.
kiusokujo ye go annai
　restingplace　to　guidance
mōshi-agero.
　do

§ 171. The word 'come!' (imp. mood) in a gradually ascending scale of respect towards the person addressed.

Koi.　　　　　　　　　To children or animals, and to
　　　　　　　　　　　servants, coolies etc. in giving
　　　　　　　　　　　short orders.

O ide.　　　　　　　　Familiar.
O ide na.
O ide nasare.　　　　　Ordinary form among equals.
Irasshare.
O ide nasaremase.　　　To superiors.
Irassharemase
O ide asobase.　　　　 To persons much superior in
　　　　　　　　　　　rank.
O ide asobashimase.　　Exceedingly respectful.

If the word 'please' is introduced, the scale will be as follows:—

　　Kite kurero.
　　Kite kure.

HONORIFIC AND HUMBLE FORMS. 181

Kite kure na.
Kite o kure.
Ki tamaye. Student's language.
Kite kudasare.
O ide kudasare.
O ide nasatte kudasare.
O ide wo negaimasŭ.
Irasshatte kudasare.
Irasshatte kudasaimase.

§ 172. CONTEMPTUOUS FORMS OF EXPRESSION.

Some nouns have a contemptuous force, as *tsura* 'mug,' for *kawo* 'face,' *yatsu* 'fellow,' for *hito* 'man.'

Examples of Contemptuous Verbs are—

Kuu or *kurau*,	'to eat'	for	*taberu.*
Useru,	'to go away'	for	*iku.*
Ketsukaru,	'to be'	for	*aru* or *oru.*

Agaru with the stems of verbs is a contemptuous auxiliary, as *kono baka yarō me nani wo nukashi-agaru?* 'What is this —— fool gabbling about?'

Me is used after nouns as a contemptuous suffix, as *chikushō me* 'beast,' *ama me* 'hussy,' *berabō me* 'scoundrel,' *yarō me* 'low fellow.'

CHAPTER XIII.

SYNTAX.

ORDER OF WORDS IN A SENTENCE.

§ 173. The first place in a Japanese sentence is occupied by the nominative case, the next by the indirect object of the verb or by a noun followed by a postposition, the third by the direct object of the verb (accusative case) and the last by the verb or the adjective in the verbal form. Ex. *Watakŭshi wa uchi ni tabako wo nomanŭ,* 'I don't smoke (lit. 'drink') tobacco in the house ;' *tenki wa sakujitsu kara atsui,* 'the weather is hot since yesterday.'

Exception. In comparisons the object with which the comparison is made is usually, but not always, put first. Ex. *Kono yama yori are wa takai,* 'this mountain is higher than that.'

§ 174. Qualifying words or phrases precede the words which they qualify. Thus :—

(a) The adjective and the verb in the attributive form precede the noun to which they belong, as *yoroshī hĭto,* 'a good man,' *kuru hĭto* 'the man who comes.'

(b) The adverb precedes the verb, adjective or adverb which it qualifies, as *goku hayaku* 'very early,' *goku hayai* 'very early,' *hayaku koi* 'come quick.'

(c) The noun followed by the possessive particle *no* or *ga* precedes the noun to which it is joined, as *hĭto no chĭkara* 'a man's strength,' *kin no tokei* 'a gold watch.'

§ 175. Particles indicating number and case, with *wa, ya, ga, mo, ka, to,* or *nagara,* come after the noun, as *yama ni* 'to the mountain,' *kore ka* 'is it this?' Roughly speaking they come in the following order :—plural particles ; *to* or *nagara* ; case signs ; *wa, ga, ya, mo,* or *ka,* but to this there are numerous exceptions.

§ 176. The signs of gender *o* and *on, me* and *men* and the honorifics *o* and *go* are put before the word to which they belong. But these are really qualifying words, and fall under the rule in § 174.

§ 177. Expressions denoting time precede expressions denoting place and a general expression precedes one that is more precise. Ex. *Itsu Kōbe ni ikimasŭ ka ?* 'When are you going to Kobe?'; *konnichi go ji ni o ide nasare,* 'come at five o'clock today.'

But this rule is by no means rigidly observed.

§ 178. Conjunctions and interrogative particles are placed at the end of the clause or sentence to which they belong. Ex. *Kane ga arimasenŭ kara,* 'because I have no money; *naze nai ka ?* 'why have you none?'

§ 179. Dependent clauses and participles precede the principal verb of the sentence.

Kane ga aru toki, kaimashō. I intend to buy some when
money is time will buy I have the money.

Furui kimono wo utte, Having sold her old clothes,
old clothes having sold she bought new ones.
atarashi no kaimashĭta.
new bought

Clauses ending in *kara* occasionally follow the principal clause of the sentence. Ex. *Giosha san, basha wo tomete kure, koko ni oritai kara,* 'Driver, please stop the carriage : I want to get down here.' But in these cases, the latter clause is really added by way of an afterthought.

INDIRECT NARRATION.

§ 180. In European languages, a sentence when reported by another person changes its form considerably. If I say 'I will go,' another person in reporting my promise, says 'he said he would go,' 'will' being changed into 'would,' and 'he' substituted for 'I.' In Japanese no change takes place, and the fact that the sentence is a quotation is indicated simply by the particle *to* placed after it. Thus 'I will go' is *iku*; 'he said he would go' is *iku to iimashita*. See *to*, p. 146.

APOSIOPESIS.

§ 181. The Japanese are very fond of breaking off a sentence in the middle leaving the remainder to be understood. This habit of theirs explains many apparent anomalies.

Examples.

O *rusu nara*, *sashi-oki de* absent if is leave *yoroshī kara* (*motte kayeruna*). is good because	If he is absent, it will be sufficient to leave it, so (don't bring it back again).
Daiku wo yonde carpenter having called (*o kure*). give	Call a carpenter.

O kure is itself an example of this practice, *nasare* being omitted after it.

Dōzō kannin shīte please patience having done (*kudasare*).	Please have patience with me.

COORDINATION.

§ 182. The Rule by which, when two or more Verbs or Adjectives are coordinated in a sentence, the last only takes the inflection or particle belonging to all, the others being put in the indefinite form, has been already explained in §§ 46 and 82.

A somewhat similar rule applies to nouns. Particles which belong to several nouns are not put with each of them, but only with the last of the number. We do not say for example *niōbō wo kodomo wo sutete nigemashĭta* but *niōbō kodomo wo sutete nigemashĭta*, 'he ran away abandoning his wife and children.'

CHAPTER XIV.

TIME, MONEY, WEIGHTS AND MEASURES.

YEARS.

§ 183. The Japanese have two modes of reckoning years. One is by means of a cycle of twelve years, to which the names of the twelve signs of the Japanese zodiac have been given. These signs are:—

    1876 *Ne*, the rat.
    1877 *Ushi*, the bull.
    1878 *Tora*, the tiger.
    1879 *U* (for *usagi*) the hare.
    1880 *Tatsu*, the dragon.
    1881 *Mi*, the serpent.
    1882 *Mŭma*, the horse.
    1883 *Hitsuji*, the goat.
    1884 *Saru*, the monkey.
    1885 *Tori*, the cock.
    1886 *Inu*, the dog.
    1887 *I*, the wild boar.
    1888 is again *Ne*, and so on.

This mode of reckoning is not much used now except in referring to the year of one's birth.

The other plan is by means of periods of uncertain length distinguished by a special name (*nengō*). These periods were formerly fixed arbitrarily, but it has been announced that in future they will coincide with the reigns of the Mikados. The present year (1888) is the 21st year of *Meiji*. The Japanese year now coincides with our own and begins on the 1st January.

TIME, MONEY, WEIGHTS AND MEASURES. 187

Months.

§ 184. The Gregorian calendar has been introduced in Japan for the month as well as for the year.

The months are called :—

January,	shō	gatsŭ.	August,	hachi gatsŭ.
February,	ni	,,	September,	ku ,,
March,	san	,,	October,	jiu ,,
April,	shi	,,	November,	jiu ichi ,, or
May,	go	,,		shimotsuki.
June,	roku	,,	December,	jiu ni gatsŭ,
July,	shichi	,,		or shiwasŭ.

'One month,' 'two months,' &c., are expressed by means of the Japanese numerals and *tsŭki*, the Japanese word for a month. 'One month' is *hĭto tsŭki*, 'two months' *fŭta tsŭki*, &c.

Ik-ka-getsŭ (contr. for *ichi-ka-getsŭ*), 'one month,' *ni-ka-getsŭ*, 'two months' etc., may also be used.

Days.

§ 185. The days of the month are as follows :—

1st,	*tsuitachi*.	17th,	*jiu shichi nichi*.
2nd,	*futsŭka*.	18th,	,, *hachi nichi*.
3rd,	*mikka*.	19th,	,, *ku nichi*.
4th,	*yokka*.	20th,	*hatsŭka*.
5th,	*itsŭka*.	21st,	*ni jiu ichi nichi*.
6th,	*muika*.	22nd,	,, ,, *ni nichi*.
7th,	*nanuka*.	23rd,	,, ,, *san nichi*.
8th,	*yōka*.	24th,	,, ,, *yokka*.
9th,	*kokonoka*.	25th,	,, ,, *go nichi*.
10th,	*tōka*.	26th,	,, ,, *roku nichi*.
11th,	*jiu ichi nichi*.	27th,	,, ,, *shichi nichi*.
12th,	,, *ni nichi*.	28th,	,, ,, *hachi nichi*.
13th,	,, *san nichi*.	29th,	,, ,, *ku nichi*.
14th,	,, *yokka*.	30th,	*san-jiu-nichi*.
15th,	,, *go nichi*.	31st,	,, ,, *ichi-nichi*.
16th,	,, *roku nichi*.		

188   TIME, MONEY, WEIGHTS AND MEASURES.

The above numerals may also be used when a number of days is meant, and not the day of the month. For 'one day' however we must say *ichi nichi* not *tsuitachi*. *Misoka* is used for the last day of the month on whatever day it may fall.

§ 186. The days of the week are :—

Sunday,	*Nichi yō bi.*
Monday,	*Getsu yō bi.*
Tuesday,	*Ka yō bi.*
Wednesday,	*Sui yō bi.*
Thursday,	*Moku yō bi.*
Friday,	*Kin yō bi*
Saturday,	*Do yō bi.*

Bi (for *hi*) 'day' is often omitted. Thus for 'Sunday' one may say either *Nichi yō bi* or *Nichi yō*.

The month is also divided into three *jun*, the first ten days being called *jōjun*, the second *chiujun*, and the third *gejun*.

HOURS.

§ 187. The Japanese have now adopted the European division of the day. For 'one o'clock' they say *ichi ji*, for 'two o'clock' *ni ji*, 'three o'clock' *san ji*, 'four o'clock'[*] *yoji* and so on. 'One hour' is *ichi-ji-kan*, 'two hours' *ni ji kan* etc. Minutes are called *fun*, and seconds *biō*. Thus 'five minutes and three seconds past six' is *roku ji go fun sam biō*.

MONEY.

§ 188. 100 *sen* = 1 *yen*.

The *yen* is a silver coin worth at the present rate of exchange about three English shillings. It is the equivalent of the Mexican dollar which has disappeared from circulation in Japan.

---

[*] See p. 37.

MEASURE OF LENGTH.

§ 189. 10 *rin*   = 1 *bu*
10 *bu*   = 1 *sun*
10 *sun* = 1 *shaku*
6 *shaku* = 1 *ken*
10 *shaku* = 1 *jō*
60 *ken* = 1 *chō*
36 *chō* = 1 *ri*

The *shaku* or *kaneshaku* may be taken as equal to one English foot. More accurately, it is 11.93 inches.

The *ken* is nearly six English feet (71.58 inches).

The *ri* is equal to 2.44034 English miles.

The *hiro* is not much used for accurate measurements. It may be taken as equal to about 5 feet, and like our 'fathom' is chiefly used in speaking of the depth of water.

For nautical purposes, the European Geographical mile (*kai-ri*) is used.

DRY GOODS MEASURE.

§ 190. For measuring dry goods, a *shaku* (called the *kujirajaku*) of 14.913 inches is used. The English yard is pretty generally known.

Japanese cotton and silk goods are usually made up in pieces of a little over $10\frac{3}{4}$ yds (*tan*) or of twice that length (*hiki*).

SUPERFICIAL OR LAND MEASURE.

§ 191. 30 *tsubo* = 1 *se*
10 *se*   = 1 *tan*
10 *tan* = 1 *chō*

The *tsubo*, which is the ordinary unit of measurement is 6 *kaneshaku* square or about 3.95 sq. yds. The *chō* is equal to 2.45 acres.

WEIGHT.

§ 192.
10 *rin* = 1 *fun*
10 *fun* = 1 *momme*
100 *momme* = *hyaku-me*
1000 *momme* = *kamme*
160 *momme* = 1 *kin*

The *fun* is equal to 5.7972 grains avoirdupois; the *kamme* to 8.2817 lbs. avoirdupois. The *hyakŭ-kin* or picul (100 *kin*) is the weight commonly used in commercial transactions with foreigners. It is equal to 132.5073 lbs. avoirdupois, but is usually taken as if the *kin* were 1⅓ lbs.

MEASURE OF CAPACITY.

§ 193.
10 *sai* = 1 *shaku*
10 *shaku* = 1 *gō*
10 *gō* = 1 *shō*
10 *shō* = 1 *to*
10 *to* = 1 *koku*

This measure is used for liquids and grain. The *shō* is .397 of a gallon. A *shō* of rice weighs about 2½ *kin*. The *koku* is used for junks' measurement. One koku is equal to about $\frac{4}{27}$ of a ton or 2½ piculs.

§ 194. All the words in the above tables, except *hiro* and *tsubo*, are of Chinese origin, and are accompanied by Chinese numerals only. See Chap. V.

CHAPTER XV.

COMMON ERRORS IN SPEAKING JAPANESE.

§ 195. The following list of errors into which he is most likely to fall may be useful to the beginner:—

The use of the honorific words and particles *o, go, masŭ* (as in *arimasŭ*), *nasaru*, (as in *o ide nasare*), and *anata* in addressing servants or coolies.

O hayō means 'early,' and should not be used late in the day without some special meaning.

Shinjō means 'respectfully to offer,' and should not be made to mean simply 'give.'

The use of the numerals *hĭtotsŭ, fŭtatsŭ*, &c. where custom requires the words described in § 32.

The use of the form of the adjective ending in *i* where that ending in *u* is required. *Yoroshi arimasŭ, warui gozaimasŭ,* are often heard instead of *yoroshiu arimasŭ, warŭ gozaimasŭ.*

The indiscriminate introduction of personal and possessive pronouns. See Chap. IV. Remember that for one of these pronouns in Japanese there are at least ten in English.

Confounding in pronunciation short and long vowels and single and double consonants.

The arrangement of the words of a sentence in a wrong order. See Chapter XIII.

CHAPTER XVI.

EXTRACTS.

The following extracts are intended chiefly to illustrate the use of honorifics. They are taken from modern Japanese novels, the conversations in which are in the colloquial style, the narrative part being in the written language. *Yenchō*'s novels, which are entirely composed in the spoken language, are an exception. *Yenchō* is the best-known public story-teller of Tokio, and an amanuensis takes down his tales exactly as he delivers them.

The number of lady students of Japanese is increasing, and it may therefore be convenient to state that the story called *Asŭkagawa*, the opening passage of which is given in Extract V., is suitable for their reading. The narrative part, however, is in the written style, and perhaps the best plan will be not to attempt to read it but to get a Japanese teacher to relate the substance of it vivâ voce.

I.

Conversation with a Jinrikisha Coolie.

Fare. *Oi! oi! Kurumaya! michi ga chigai wa shinai ka?*
       I say   jinriksha man road   mistake   not do ?
Coolie. *He, he, daijōbu de gozaimasŭ.* F. *Doko ye ikunda*
          quite safe   is   where to go is
(for *iku no da*) *ka shitte oru ka?* C. *He, zonjite orimasŭ:*
        ? knowing remain ?   knowing remain
kochira kara mairimashĭta hō ga chikai no de gozaimasŭ (gara
this way from   came   side   near   is   rattle
gara gara). F. *Oi! oi! Daga, doko da ka shitteru*
rattle rattle   I say   But where is ? knowing remain

EXTRACTS. 193

.ka? C. He, he, zonjite orimasŭ. (gara gara). F. Zonjite
?   knowing remain   rattle rattle   knowing
oru   ja (for de wa) wakaranai.   Doko ye ikunda ? C.
remain with   is not intelligible where to go is
He, he (gara gara). F. Kore!   matte   kure to   iu
        rattle rattle   this having waited give that saying
ni. (gara gara gara gara gara gara).
in   rattle rattle rattle rattle rattle rattle

From a Japanese novel called *Shosei katagi*.

TRANSLATION.

Fare. I say, jinriksha man! are not you going the wrong way?
Coolie. Yes, Sir, it is all right, Sir. F. Do you know where you
are going? Yes, Sir, I know, this is the short road (rattle, rattle).
F. I say, but do you know where it is (I am going)? C. Yes,
Sir, I know. (rattle, rattle). F. I don't understand what you
mean with your 'I know.' Where is it you are going? C. Yes,
Sir (rattle, rattle). F. Look here! wait, I tell you. (rattle, rattle,
rattle, rattle, rattle, rattle).

II.

A Lady Teacher is informed by one of her pupils that
a gentleman of rank has come to pay her a visit.

Pupil. O shishō sama ye mōshi-agemasŭ.   Tadaima Yagi-
        teacher   say raise   just now
wara sama ga o ide ni narimashita ga,   o ima   ye o tōshi
              come   became   sitting room   pass
mōshimashō   ka? Teacher. E,   nani ?   Yagiwara sama
(humble auxiliary) ?   eh   what
ga.... O, sayō desŭ ka?   Ima   yori   wa ano oku no
        oh so   is it ?   sitting-room rather than   back
ko-zashiki ye go   annai   mōshi-agete kudasai. Sore kara
small-parlour   invitation (humble aux.) please   that after
suye   ye iitsŭkete, o tomo no   shiu   ni mo go shiu wo dashite,
servant to ordering suite of persons to too   sake   put out
      oku   ye mo itsumo no   o riōri   wo o mochi
back part of the house   always of cooked food   take
nasai yo. Hayaku nasaranŭ to (ikenai) o isogi ka mo zonji-
            soon   do not   if   haste ? even not
masenŭ yo.
know

Shinsō no gajin.

TRANSLATION.

Pupil. Madam, I beg to inform you that Mr. Yagiwara has just arrived. Shall I show him into the sitting-room? Teacher, Eh! what? Mr. Yagiwara has ...... Is that so? Don't show him into the sitting-room but into the small reception room at the back of the house. Then tell the servants to let the people of his suite have some sake, and being the usual refreshments to the back part of the house. You must be quick about it, for he may perhaps be in a hurry.

Note the highly respectful forms *sama, mōshi-ageru*, used by the pupil to the teacher, and the honorific references to the guest by the use of *sama, o ide ni naru, o tūshi mōshimashō, go annai, o riōri* and *o isogi*. The teacher's language to the pupil differs from that used to a servant as the forms *desŭ, kudasai, o machi nasai, nasaranŭ* and *zonjimasenŭ* show. It has an air of friendly condescension.

III.

A young man of the lower class meets a merchant's son as the latter is going to the bath-house.

A. *Toki ni waka-danna! kore kara go niutō ni natte,*
time   young master this from   enter bath having become

sore kara dō nasaru no desŭ? B. *Uchi ye kayeru no sa.* A. *O*
that from how do   is   house to return

uchi ye o kayeri ni natte, sore kara? B. *Asameshi wo*
house to return having become that from   morning rice

kuu no yo. A. *Asa gozen wo meshi-agatte, sore kara?*
eat   morning meal having-partaken of that from

B. *Urusai nā; mise ni itte, akinai wo suru no sa.* A.
bothersome shop to having gone business do

Naruhodo: sono o akinai wo shite hi ga kureru
become quantity that business having done sun go down

to? B. *Yū-meshi wo kuu no sa.* A. *Sono go yūhan ga*
when evening rice eat   that evening meal

sumu to, dō nasaimasŭ? B. *Mise no wakai mono wo aite*
finish when how do   shop young person partner

ni (shite) hanashi demo suru no sa. A. *Sono hanashi ga sumu*
talk even do   that talk   finish

to? B. *Urusai nā. hoka ni shikata mo nai kara,*
when bothersome! else do-side even is not because

neru no sa.
go to bed

Meiji uki yo no furo.

EXTRACTS. 195

TRANSLATION.

A. Well but—young master! You are now going to have a bath. After that what will you do? B. I shall go home. A. When you have gone home, what next? B. I shall have my breakfast. A. And when you have had your breakfast, what then? B. You are a nuisance, I go to the shop and attend to business. A. To be sure. And when business is over, and the sun goes down? B. I have my supper. A. And when supper is finished, what do you do? B. I very likely have a talk with the youug men in the shop. A. And when your talk is over? B. You are a nuisance. Then there is nothing else to be done but to go to bed.

IV.

Interview with a ragman.

Ragman. *Kudzuya de gozai*; *kudzu wa o harai wa gozaimasenŭ*
      ragman   it is   rags   sell   is not
ka? Customer. *Choito! kudzu ya san! kore wo totte*
?   a little   ragman Mr. this having taken
o kure. R. *He, he! haiken itashimashō; zuibun*
  give   yes   look (respectful) will do   tolerably
furubite soshite yogorete imasŭ na. He ;
having become old and having become dirty is
ikahodo ni itadakimasŭ? C. *Omaye mā funde goran*
how much for receive   you having estimated see
yo. R. *He, he, hassen de wa ikaga sama?* C. *Bakana koto*
               eight sen with how   foolish thing
o ii de nai yo. Sore demo moto wa takakŭ te kirei
say is not   that with even originally dear and pretty
d'atta yo; sonnani fumi-taosarete tamaru mono ka
was   so much estimate being knocked down endure thing ?
ne? R. *He; moto wa takaku te kirei ni chigai arimasenŭ*
          originally dear   pretty mistake is not
ga; kore ga chirimen nareba koso hassen
but this   crape because it is (emphatic part.) eight sen
ni mo itadakimasŭ; sore de nakereba dō shĭte he.
for receive (humble) that for were-it-not how having done
C. *Atarimaye da ne; da kara watai mo hassen de wa iyada*
   ordinary it is is because I too eight sen for   dislike
to iunda, ne: jiu go sen ni o shi; sore de omaye ni son wa nai
  saying is   fifteen sen   do that with you to loss is not

yo.   R. *Dō   itashimashĭte—sore   ja   maido   nega-*
(emphatic part.)   how   having done   well then every   time re-
un'desŭ   kara,   jissen ni itadakimashō.   He, sore de yoroshĭku-
questing is because   ten sen   will receive   that with if good
ba he. C. *Shikata ga nai ne;   motte   o ide yo.*   R. *Arigatō*
              do-side   is not   having taken   go   thank
zonjimasŭ: chōdo jissen;   maido   arigatō zonjimasŭ.   Kudzu ya
you   exactly ten sen every time   thank you   ragman
de gozai.   C. *Ingō na kudzu ya da ne.*   R. *Kudzu wa o harai de*
it   is   hard   ragman   rags   sell

gozarimasenŭ ka?
   is not

Kudzu ya no kago.

TRANSLATION.

Ragman. (calls) The Ragman! Any rags for sale!

Customer. I say, ragman! won't you take this?

Yes, Ma'am! please let me see it; it is pretty old, and dirty besides; yes, Ma'am! how much shall I give you for it?

Do you put a price on it.

Yes, Ma'am. Would eight cents?

Don't talk nonsense; that was a very pretty and expensive thing when it was new and I can't let it go for so little as that.

Yes, Ma'am! No doubt it was a pretty and expensive thing when it was new, and it is just because it is crape that I will take it from you for eight sen, otherwise I really—

Well, I suppose you have a right to name your price, but I would have you know that I have something to say to it too and I won't take eight sen. Make it fifteen sen; you will lose nothing by it.

Really, Ma'am, I could'nt think——. Well then, as you are such a good customer, I will take it from you for ten sen. If that will suit you—

Well! it can't be helped, take it away.

Thank you, Ma'am, (here is your money)—just ten sen. Much obliged for all your custom. (calls) The Ragman!

How fond that ragman is of a hard bargain!

Any rags for sale! Exit.

V.

A young engaged couple view the plum blossoms and listen to the nightingale.*

She (from the garden).	*Takeo*	*san!*	*Takeo san!*		*chotto.*
	(personal name) Mr.				a moment
He (from the house).	*Nani ka*	*arimashita*	*ka?;*	*ima*	*iku tokoro*
	anything	was	?	now	go place
desŭ. (comes out). She.	*Ima*	*mukō*	*no*	*mŭmebayashi*	*de*
it is.	now	opposite		plum grove	in
uguisu	*no hatsu ne ga shĭta*	*yō*	*desŭ*	*kara,*	*kiki ni*
nightingale	first note did	manner	is	because	hear to
ikimashō. He.	*Sayō desŭ ka.*	*Sore wa*	*yukai*	*desŭ na:*	*sā,*
let us go	thus it is ?	that	pleasant	is	come
itte	*kikimashō.* (A little later).	*O jō san!*	*anata wa o*
having gone	let us hear	Miss	you
damashi de wa arimasenŭ ka?	*Chitto mo*	*uguisu*	*ga naki-*
deceiving is not ?	a little even	nightingale	sings
masenŭ ne. She.	*Iye,*	*sakki*	*yoi ne*	*wo*	*shĭte,*	*futa*
not	no	a while ago	good voice		having done	two
koye bakari nakimashĭta	*kara*	*anata wo o yobi mōshĭta no desŭ.*
cries only sang	because	you call did is
He.	*Sō desŭ ka?*	*Shikashi*	*nan'da*	*ka*	*ate*	*ni nara-*
	it is so ?	but	somehow		reliance	not
nai	*yō*	*na*	*ki*	*ga shimasŭ ne.*	She. *Mattaku*
become	manner		mind	does	completely
sakki	*naita*	*koto*	*wa*	*nakimashĭta*	*kara*	*sŭkoshi*
a while ago	sung	thing		sung	because	a little
matte	*ite*	*mimashō.*	He. *Sonnara kore kara mō*	*ichiji*
waiting	remaining	will see	if so this from more	one hour
kan	*hodo*	*matte*	*nakanakattara dō nasaimasŭ.*	She. *Sō*
space	amount	waiting	if should not sing how do	so
desŭ ne.	*Kō shimashō.*	*Nan'daka hinata ye*	*detara*
it is	thus will do	what is it sunshine to	since went out
nodo ga	*kawaita*	*yō*	*desŭ kara,*	*kahe wo ii-tsŭke*
throat	became dry	appearance	it is because	coffee order
ni iku	*o tsukai wo shimashō.*	He. *Sorewa omoshiroi.*	*Watakŭshi*
to go	your messenger will do	that is amusing	I
mo nanda ka nomi mono ga hoshiku	*natta*	*tokoro desŭ kara—*
too what is it drink thing desirous	have become	place is because
She. *Sore de*	*watakŭshi no o yaku wa*	*dekimashĭta ga;*	*moshi*
that with	my office	has been made	if

---

* The *uguisu* is not a nightingale but a bird somewhat resembling it.

naitara   anata wa dō nasaimasŭ. He. *Sō desŭ ne.   Naitara*
it should sing you   how   do   so it is   if should sing
watakŭshi mo sono   o tsukai   ni ikimashō. She. *Sore wa ikema-*
    I   .also   your messenger as   will go   that   won't
senŭ yo. Sono koto wa watakŭshi ga kangayeta no desŭ   kara.
do •   that thing   I   thought of   is because
He. *Sonnara nan'demo   o nozomi no koto wo shimashō.* She.
    if so anything at all your wish   thing   will do
Sakki   mite o ide nasatta watashi no namayerashi   mono
a while ago reading you were   my   name resembling   thing
no atta ano o tegami wo o mise nasai na. He. *Yō gozaimasŭ;*
    was that letter   show   good   it is
moshi naitara   o me   ni kakemashō. She. *Kitto desu ka?*
 if   it should sing your eyes on will hang   certain it is ?
He. *Kitto   o me ni kakemasŭ to mo.* She. *Ima ga   sakari*
    certainly eyes on will hang   now   full blossom
desŭ ne. He. *Sō desŭ, ima ga chōdo midokoro desŭ ga, jitsu ni*
 is   so it is now   exactly see-place it is   truly
mŭme wa hoka no hana to chigatte   hin ga yoi   kara
plum   other   flowers from differing quality is good because
miru hito no kokoro   made   shizen to kōshō ni naru
see person   heart   as far as   naturally elevated   become
yō   desŭ ne. She. *Sayō de gozaimasŭ.   Hito no   kōsai*
manner it is   thus   it is   people   intercourse
mo kore to onaji-koto de watashi nado mo kō shite anataga-
also this as same thing being I   etc. also thus doing   you
ta no yōna o   kata   to   shijin o tsuki-ai wo shite iru
    kind of gentleman with constantly   association   doing
no de jibun no ichi   ga shizen to agaru ka to omoimasŭ yo.
    by own   position   naturally   rises ?   think
He. *Dō   shite; watakŭshi nado wa sonna wake ni wa mai-*
     how having done   I   etc.   such reason ·   do
rimasenŭ ga: nan'de mo hito wa tomodachi wo yerabu no ga
not go (pause) anyhow   people · friends   choosing
kanjin desŭ. Toki ni, o jō san! tsŭkanai koto wo o kiki
important is   by the way Miss   not stick   thing   inquire
mōshimasŭ ga, kono maye no Nichiyō mo ima no Nichiyō mo
(humble aux.)   this before   Sunday   now   Sunday also
Daijin   wa nanika   o shirabe mono no   yō   desŭ
His Excellency   something   investigation   appearance is
ga, o kajimuki no o   shirabe   desŭ ka. She. *Iye, watashi mo*
    household   investigation is ?   no   I   too
yoku wa   shirimasenŭ   ga, anata mo go zonji no tōri
well   do not know but   you too   know   manner

mai-toshi   kono mūmc no   sakari   ni wa   yenkai   wo
every year   this plum   full bloom at   entertainment

itashimasŭ kara   kono aida   haha ga sono koto wo mōshi-
does   because   the other day mother   that thing   when

mashĭtara,   ko-toshi   wa   ayaniku   shirabe-mono ga aru
she spoke of this year   unfortunately   investigation   is

kara   yenkai   wa gozarimasenŭ to kotayemashĭta.
because entertainment   is not   answered

Asŭkagawa.

TRANSLATION.

She. (from the garden) Takeo! come here for a little.

He. (from the house) what is it? I'll be with you in a moment. (he comes out).

I thought just now I heard the first song of the nightingale from the plum orchard over there: let us go and listen to it.

Indeed. How nice! Come! we will go and hear it. (a little later) Have you not been humbugging me, Miss? The nightingale does not sing a bit.

Yes, a while ago, it did sing twice with a beautiful note, and that was why I called you.

Indeed! But somehow I don't feel quite satisfied.

It did really sing a while ago, so let us wait a little and see.

Well then, we'll wait for an hour from now, and if it does not sing by that time, what will you do?

Well, I'll tell you what I will do. Coming out into the sun makes me thirsty, so I will go and order a cup of coffee for you.

That is a good idea. I do feel as if I should like something to drink.

Now that it is settled what I have got to do, if the nightingale does sing, what will you do?

Certainly. If it sings, I will go as your messenger.

That will never do: that was my idea.

Well then, I will do anything you like.

Show me the letter you were reading a while ago which had something like my name in it.

Very good; if it sings, I will show it to you.

You promise me faithfully.

I promise faithfully to show it to you.

The plum-trees are just now in full blossom.
Yes, now is exactly the time to see them. Indeed the plum is of a quality so far surpassing other flowers that it naturally elevates as it were the minds of those who look on it.
You are right. And it is the same with the society one keeps; I feel as if the position of a person like myself were naturally raised by constant association in this way with gentlemen like you.
Not at all! that is not so in my case. Still people ought to be very careful in their choice of friends. By the way, Miss! to change the subject, I want to ask you a question. Both last Sunday and today His Excellency seems to have been engaged in investigating something; is it some private matter?
No, I really do not quite know, but as you will remember, he has been in the habit of giving an entertainment every year when the plnm-trees are in full blossom. When my mother asked him about it the other day, he said that unfortunately he would be prevented from giving it this year by an investigation which he had in hand.

VI.
A man of high rank talks to a newly-engaged servant.

Master. *Kore! kore! Temaye wa Kōdzuke to mōsu ka?*
　　　　 this　 this　 you　　　　　　　　　　 are called　?

Servant. *Hei,　Tonosama　ni wa gokigen yoroshiu—watakŭshi*
　　　　 yes　 your Lordship　 health　 good　　　 I

wa Kōdzuke to mōshimasŭ　 shinzan　 mono　 de gozaimasŭ.
　　 called　　　　　　　　 new came　 person　 　 am

M. *Sono hō wa shinzan　 mono demo　kage　hinata　　naku*
　 you　　　 new come person　even　shade sunshine without-

yoku hataraku to itte,　daibu　　 hiōban　yoku mina
distinction well　work　 saying a good deal reputation well　all

no uke　　 ga yoi yo. Toshigoro wa ni jiu　ichi　ni to miyeru
reception　is good　　　 age　　　 twenty one or two　　 seem

ga,　 hito-gara　　　to ii,　 otokoburi　 to ii,　 zōri-tori ni wa
　　personal appearance say manly bearing　say　 sandals take as

oshi　　　　 mono da. S. Tonosama　ni wa　　 konaida-jiu　　go
regrettable thing is　　 your Lordship　　　 for some days past

fukai　　　　de gozaimashĭta　 sō de　　o　　　　anji-mōshi-
indisposition　 having been　 appearance　by feel anxious

agemashĭta   ga;   sashĭ-taru   koto   mo   gozaimasenŭ   ka.
did (humble)   (pause)   important   thing   is not   ?

M. *O, yoku   tadzunete   kureta;   betsu   ni sashĭtaru   koto   mo*
  oh well   having asked gave   specially   important thing even

nai   ga.   Shĭte—temaye wa ima made idzukata ye   hōkō   wo
it is not (pause). And   you   now until   where   service

shĭta koto ga atta ka? S. *Hei! Tadaima made   hōbō   hōkō   mo*
did thing   was   Yes   just now until all quarters service

itashimashĭta — madzu   ichi-ban saki ni Yotsuya no kanamonoya
have done   to begin with   first-of-all   ironmonger

ye mairimashĭta ga, ichi nen   hodo   orimashĭte,   kake-dashima-
    went   but one year amount having remained   ran away

shĭta; sore kara Shimbashi no   kajiya   ye mairi,   mi   tsŭki
  that after   blacksmith   going   three months

hodo   sugite   kake-dashi, mata Nakadōri no Yezōshiya   ye
amount having passed ran away again   picture dealer

mairimashĭta ga,   tōka   de kake-dashimashĭta. M. *Sono hō no*
  went   but ten days with ran away   you

yō ni   sō   akite   wa hōkō wa dekinai yo. S. *Watakŭshi ga*
manner so getting tired service   cannot do   I

akippoi   no de wa gozaimasenŭ   ga,   watakŭshi   wa
readily disgusted   am not   (pause)   I

dōzō   shĭte   buke   hōkō ga itashĭtai to   omoi,
some how or another military house service   wish to do   thinking,

sono wake wo oji ni tanomimashĭtemo,   oji wa buke hōkō wa
that reason uncle having applied even   uncle

mendō da kara,   chōka   ye ike   to mōshimashĭte,
trouble is because merchant's house to go (imp.)   having said

achi   kochi   hōkō ni yarimasu   kara,   watakŭshi mo tsura-
thither hither   service   sends   because   I   too face

ate   ni   kake-dashĭte   yarimashĭta. M. *Sono hō wa*
hit by way of having run away   gave   you

kiukutsu na buke hōkō wo   shitai   to in   mono wa ikaga na
irksome   wish to do   said thing   how

wake   ja? S. *Hei; watakŭshi wa   buke   hōkō wo itashi,*
reason   I   military house   doing

o kenjutsŭ wo. oboyetai   no de, hei. M. *Ha! kenjutsu-suki*
fencing   wish to learn   by   ·   ah   fencing like

to nā.

Botan dōrō by Yenchō.

TRANSLATION.

Master. Look here! Is your name Kōdzuke?

Servant. Yes, Sir, My name is Kōdzuke, I have just entered your Lordship's service; I hope your Lordship is in good health.

I hear that though you are a new comer you have made a favourable impression on everybody, and that you have got a good character for working hard night and day. You seem about twenty one or twenty two years of age, and with your looks and bearing, it is a pity you are nothing better than a sandal bearer.

I understand that your Lordship has been unwell for some days past, and I was anxious about you; I hope it is nothing serious.

Thank you, it is nothing of importance. And where have you been at service up to now?

Up to the present, I have been at service in various places. First of all I went to an ironmonger's in Yotsuya, and after being there three years I ran away: then I went to a blacksmith's in Shimbashi. I ran away from him after three months. I next took service with a picture-dealer in Nakadori St, but I left him in ten days.

But you can't do your duty as a servant if you get disgusted in that way.

Oh! It is not that I am easily disgusted; it is because I wanted to take service in the house of some military noble. I begged my uncle to get me a situation of this kind, but he told me that service with a military noble was very troublesome, and that I must go to a merchant's. So he sent me to service here and there, and I ran away just to spite him.

But what made you want to take employment with a military noble? It is an irksome kind of service.

Well, Sir, It was in order that I might learn fencing.

Ah! You say you are fond of fencing?

VII.

A youth named Tasŭke goes to the Toda yashiki to ask for his father. He addresses the officer in charge of the gate.

Tasūke. *Hai! Gomen nasai.* Officer. *Doko ye mairunda? Mono-*
        pardon do   where   are going   beg-
morai nara achira ye ike. T. *Hai. Shūshō mono ga uketamawa-*
gar if are thither go   little thing   wish to

ritō   gozaimasŭ.   O.   Mono ga   kikitakereba   o   tsuji   ye   ike.
learn   am   if wish to hear outer guard   go
Nanda?   kojiki   mita   yō   na   nari   wo   shĭte—T.   *Kore   kara   kojiki*
what   beggar   seen   kind   of   dress   this   from beggar
ni   nareba   narunda   ga,   mada   kojiki   ni   wa   naranai.   Ano—
if become   is becoming   but   yet   beggar   ot-become
Toda   sama   no o   yashĭki   wa   koko   de   gozaimasŭ   ka?   O.
                       daimio's residence   here   is   ?
Toda   sama   no yashĭki   wa   kochi   da.   T.   *Sore   de   wa   jiu yo   nen*
                                   here is   then   fourteen years
maye   ni   kochi ye   kakayerareta Shiobara Kakuyemon *to   iu   kata   ga*
before   here   employed   person
arimasŭ   ka?   O.   *Nani?*   Shiobara?   *hai, are   wa   jiu san   nen   maye*
is.   what   he   thirteen years before
ni   shĭta-dzume   ni   natte,   kono   o   yashĭki   ni   wa
country-station   having become   this
oranŭ.   T.   *O kuni   wa   Yashiu no Utsunomiya de gozaimasŭ*
does not live   province   Kōdzuke   is
ka?   O.   *Maye   wa Utsunomiya de   atta   ga,* Matsudaira Tonomo
?   before   was but
no kami dono to o   kuni-kaye   ni   natte,   ima de wa Hi-
                         province change   having become now
zen   no Shimabara *da.*   T.   Hizen *no* Shimabara *to   iu   tokoro   wa*
           is   place
tō   gozaimasŭ ka?   O.   *Sō sa.* Shimabara *made   wa,   sam*
distant   is   ?   yes   as far as   three
biaku   ichi ri   han aru na.   (Tasŭke falls down in a faint.)
hundred one   half is
O.   *Kore! kore!   achi   ye maire!   achi   ye maire.*
        this   this   thither   go

Shiobara Tasŭke
by *Yenichō.*

TRANSLATION.

Tasŭke. Excuse me. Officer. Where are you going ? If you have come to beg, get away. T. I want to inquire something from you. O. If you want to inquire, you can go to the outer guard. What do you mean, you beggarly looking fellow ? T. If after this I am to become a beggar, I suppose I shall become one, but I have not got so far yet. Is this the residence of Lord Toda ? O. Yes, it is Lord Toda's residence. T. Then is there a gentleman here named Shiobara Kakuyemon who entered this service fourteen years ago ? O. What ? Shiobara ? yes, he went on duty to our province thirteen years ago, and does not live here now. T. Your province is Utsunomiya in Kōdzuke, is it not? O. It was Utsunomiya formerly, but there was an exchange of domain with Lord Matsudaira Toriomo no kami, and now it is Shimabara in Hizen. T. Is Shimabara in Hizen far off? O. That it is. It is three hundred and one ri and a half to Shimabara. (Tasŭke falls down in a faint.) O. Here! here! Be off with you. Be off with you.

VIII.
Dreams.

A. *Yume de   matsu-jo   ga zommei shite   iru   yōsu*
   dream in youngest daughter alive doing remain appearance
wo   mite,   kokoro ga mayoimashite ne, ika naru dōri to mo
having seen heart   being bewildered   how be rationale
kai   shi kanemasŭ ga;   zentai Shina de mōsŭ yō   ni
understand do cannot (pause) generally China in say manner by
seimu   nazo to iu   koto ga gozaimashō ka na? Ninna san
true dream (plur.) called thing   will be   ?   (surname)
wa   tetsugakuka   da to uketamawatta   kara,   futo   go
student of philosophy is   learnt   because suddenly
shitsumon wo itasŭ wake desŭ ga—
interrogation do reason it is (pause)

B. *Naruhodo, soriya hanahada kitai na o yume ni wa sōi*
    indeed   that   very   strange   dream   mistake
nai   ga—shikashi   korai   sono   rei   wa amata aru
is not (pause) but from old time of that precedent plenty is
koto de,   nani   mo   kikai na koto ja arimasenŭ yo. Sci-
thing being anything miraculous thing   is not   true
mu no gotoki wa moto yori mōtō arubekarazaru dōri   de,
dream the like of of course a jot ought not to be principle being
somo-somo yume to iu mono wa ika nara mono ka to   iu
this being so dream called thing how being thing ?   saying
ni   kedashi   waga   kokoro no hataraki ni hoka nara-
in pretty nearly one's own mind   operation than other does not
zu   desŭ. Yoru ni naru to ningen no shintai wa hiruma no
become is   night becomes human   body   daytime
tsŭkare   de   ne-itte   shimai, maru de kan-
fatigue on account of having fallen asleep finish wholly sensa-
kaku ga naku narimasŭ ga, nō wa mattaku shintai to chigatte
tion   not becomes but brain   wholly body from differing
yoru to iyedomo kiusoku sezu shite hiru no tōri ni hataraki-
night although rest not do doing day of manner in works
masŭ kara,   nō ga odayaka   de   nai toki nanzo
because brain   quiet (sign of pred.) is not time (plural part.)

wa	koto	ni iroiro na	koto wo	mirun'de	arimasŭ.	Katsu ya
	particularly	all kinds of thing		seeing(pred.)	is	farther

kankaku ga yasun'de   iru   no de gwaibu kara no   shigeki
sensation   resting remaining   by outside from   impression
ga sŭkoshi mo   nai   kara,   shĭtagatte   mokuzen   no
 a little even is not   because, accordingly eye-before
koto   wo   kangayeru   hitsuyō mo   naku,   shizen
thing   reflect upon   necessity   is not   naturally
omoi-yoranŭ mukashi no koto nado yume de wa miru koto ga
not think of ancient   thing (plur.) dream   in   see thing
arimasŭ no sa. Kore ta nashi.   Sōjite   ningen   to iu
   is   this other is not on the whole mankind called
mono wa yōshū no toki kara no   keiken   wo ba minna nōzui
thing   infancy   time from   experience   all   brain
no uchi ni   osamete   tsune   ni takuwayete wa orimasŭ
within   having laid up ordinarily   stored   remains
no da ga, hiru wa mi-kiki suru koto ga ōkute   sore ya kore
 is but   day   see hear do thing   being many that this
ya ni   tori-magirete mokuzen no koto ni muyō-na shisō wa
by being confused   eye-before thing for needless thought
 shizen   oku   no hō ye hiki-komi-gachi ni natte   yōi ni
naturally back part   side   retire   having become readily
omoidasŭ mono de arimasenŭ.   Tatoye   wo motte kore wo
think of   thing (pred.) is not   illustration   taking this
mōseba — yōriu kage kurō shĭte keika no   san-taru wo miru ga
if one say willow shade dark   firefly shine   see
gotoku,   yashoku   chin-chin to shĭte hajimete mushi no koye wo
 like   night-colour quiet   first   insect   cry
kiku to   ippan,   hotaru wa hiruma   oranŭ   mono de mo
hear   same thing firefly   day time not remain thing even
naku, mushi wa hiru nakanŭ mono de   mo nai ga,   hiru wa
is not insect   day not cry thing   even is not but   day
sŭzōshĭ yuye hoka no shigeki ni   sasayerarete   go-jin ga
noisy because other impressions   being impeded I+man=we
ki ga tsukanŭ   dōri   de arimasŭ. Desŭ kara yume to iu
mind not stick principle   it is   it is because dream called
mono wa to ni kaku   katsŭte   omotte   otta koto wo miru
thing in-any-case previously having thought put thing   see
mon' de kesshĭte omowanai koto wo miru mon' de arimasenŭ yo.
thing being certainly not think thing   see thing   is not

The above passage is in a much less familiar style than the others. It contains numerous expressions and forms which are only used by educated men or in books.

From the *Shosei Katagi*.

TRANSLATION.

A. Having seen in a dream my youngest daughter as if alive, my mind is quite perplexed, and I cannot understand on what principle this could take place. Is it possible that there may be after all such things as true dreams, as they say in China? I hear that you, Mr. Ninna, are a student of philosophy, and it amounts to subjecting you without warning to an examination—(but I should like to know your opinion).

B. Indeed. That is unquestionably a very strange dream. But there are numerous precedents of such dreams from old times, and there is nothing miraculous about it. In principle there can of course be no such thing as 'true dreams.' This being so, let me explain the nature of what we call dreams. It may be taken that they are neither more nor less than the operation of one's own mind. At night, the human body, owing to the fatigue of the day, falls asleep, and all sensation ceases. But the mind, unlike the body, does not rest even at night. It continues its activity as in the daytime. The brain therefore, when it is unquiet, is specially sensitive to all manner of things, and as sensation is suspended, there are no impressions from without. There is therefore no necessity for it to attend to that which is immediately before it, and so in dreams we naturally become conscious of past things which we had not been thinking of. The sole reason for this is that mankind generally are from their infancy continually receiving and storing up all their experiences in their brains. In the daytime, owing to the multitude of impressions, our minds become confused by one thing and another, and thoughts needless for immediate matters are huddled back into the interior of the mind from whence they are not readily brought out again by reflection. As an illustration of this, I may quote the saying: 'It is in the dark shade of the willow that we can best see the lustre of the firefly; it is not until night, when all is still, that we can hear the cries of the insects.' It is not that there are no fireflies in the daytime, or that the insects do not utter their note by day, but our minds do not attend to them owing to their being embarrassed by other impressions caused by the noises of daytime.

Hence what we call dreams are visions of things which we must have previously thought of, and we certainly can not dream of things that have never entered our minds before.

	PAGE		PAGE
A	18, 23	*Ba* (with Adj.)	98
Abstract Noun	10, 101	Because	162
Achi	18	Before	162
Adjective	5, 93	*Beki*	103
Adverb	94, 157	*Boku*	11
Again	181	Both	33, 35
Agglutination	43	But	162
Aitsu	14, 18	Can	162
All	33	Capacity, measure of	190
Alternative Form	60	Case	8
Although	161	Causative Verbs	81
Anata	12, 15, 18, 23	*Cha*	103
And	161	Chinese Words	6
Anna	18	Come	180
Annani	18	Compounds	50
Ano	18, 23	,, Formation of	4
Ano hito	14, 15	Compound Nouns	50
Ano o kata	14, 15, 29	,, Tenses	86
Anybody	29	Comparison	106
Anything	29	Concessive form of Adj.	100
Anywhere	30	,, Particle	61
Aposiopesis	184	,, Past	61
Are	14, 18	Conditional form of Adj.	100
Areru	85	,, Past	57
Aru	108	,, of Verb	76
As	162	Conjugation	42, 44, 45
Attributive Form	98	,, Common forms	87
Auxiliary Nouns	113	,, of uninflected	
,, Numerals	36	words used as Adj.	105
,, Verbs	118	Conjunctions	160
Ba (conditional) *Ba* (hypo-		Contemptuous Forms	181
thetical)	68, 76	Coördination	184

	Page		Page
Could	162	Dry Goods Measure	189
Da	18, 25	Dzutsu	121
Dachi	143	E	see ye
Daga	125	Each other	31
Danna	13	English Words into Japanese	161
Dano	118	Errors in speaking do	191
Dare	18, 25	Extracts	192
Dare de mo	29	Fractions	39
Dare ka	29	Future	69
Dare mo	29	Ga	16, 72, 122
Days	187	Gata	14, 173
De (negative)	66	Gena	126
De (particle)	119	Gender	7
Declension of Nouns	8	Go (hon. prefix.)	171
Demo	121	Go (hon. suffix.)	175
Demonstratives	18	Go-jiu-on	1
Dependent Clauses	183	Gozaru, Gozarimasŭ	172
Derivative Adj.	101	Hadzu	113
" Nouns	10	He	14
" Verbs	78	Hers	16
Desiderative Adj.	102	His	16
Desŭ	109	Hito	32
Do (pronominal)	18, 24, 26	Honorific and Humble Words	166
Do (concessive)	77	Honorific Nouns	167
Dochi	18	Honorific Prefixes	167, 171
Dŭka	26	Honorific Suffixes	173
Dokka	30	Hours	188
Doko	26	How	33
Dokodemo	30	Hypothetical Form	68
Domo	173	Hypothetical Past	57
Don	174	I	11
Donata	26	Idzure	26
Donna	18	If	162
Donnani	18	Ika	33
Dono	18, 174	Ikken	14
Dore	18, 26	Iku	33
Dore mo	29	Imperative Mood	75
Dore de mo	29	Indefinite Form of Adj.	94
Dōzō	26	Indefinite Form of Verb	50

HAZU NECESSITY

INDEX.

	PAGE		PAGE
Indefinite Pronouns ..	.. 29	*Kun*	.. 174
Indicative Present	.. 71	*Kuru*	.. 46
Indirect Narration	.. 184	Land Measure ..	.. 189
Interjections	.. 160	Length, measure of ..	.. 189
Interrogatives	.. 18	Letter Changes in Conjugation.	46
Irregular Verbs ..	.. 46	*Made*	.. 130
Iru	55, 110	*Mai*	.. 74
It	.. 14	*Masu*	.. 175
Itsu	.. 33	*Masu*, Conjugation of	46, 49
Iu	.. 112	May	.. 163
Jibun	.. 30	*Me*	.. 181
Jishin	.. 30	*Me* (gender)	7, 183
Ka 18, 19, 25, 29,	126	*Men*	7, 183
Kahodo	.. 20	Might	.. 163
Kaku	.. 20	*Mina*	.. 33
Kara	128, 183	Mine	.. 16
Kara position of ..	.. 183	*Mo* 29, 77,	131
Kano	18, 25	Money	.. 188
Kare	14, 18, 25	*Mono*	.. 115
Kayō	.. 19	Months	.. 187
Kereba	.. 100	*Mōsu*	.. 170
Keredo	.. 112	Must	65, 163
Keredo with Adj. ..	.. 101	*N* final	.. 1
Keredo with Verb ..	61, 67, 77	*Na*	18, 27
Keru	.. 112	*Na* (neg. imp.) ..	.. 74
Kimi	.. 13	*Na* (with adj.)	.. 105
Kisama	.. 13	*Na* (for *nasare*) ..	.. 75
Kū	.. 20	*Nagara*	.. 132
Ko	18, 19	*Nai* 62, 69,	98
Kochi	.. 19	*Nambo*	.. 27
Koitsu	.. 19	*Nanda*	.. 63
Koko	.. 19	*Nani*	18, 27
Konata 13, 18, 19,	23	*Nani de mo*	.. 30
Konna	.. 19	*Nanihodo*	18, 27
Konnani	.. 19	*Nanika*	.. 29
Kono	.. 19	*Nanimo*	.. 29
Kore	.. 19	*Nara*	.. 58
Koto	10, 113	*Naru*	.. 110
Koso	.. 129	*Nasaru*	75, 110

INDEX.

	Page
Ne	160
Neba	66
Nedo	66
Negative Adjective	65, 69, 102
,, Base	61
,, Concessive	66
,, Conditional	65
,, Emphatic Tenses	51
,, Future	74
,, Hypothetical	66
,, Imperative	74
,, Participle	66
,, Past	63
,, Present	62
Nengo	186
Ni	133
Nigori	4
No	99, 137
No ni	99
Noun	5
Number	7, 42
Numerals	34
Nushi	13
O	7, 10, 171, 183
O (Term. of Future)	70
Ohayō	191
Oira	11
Omaye	13, 15, 16
On	7
One	32
One's own	30
Onore	30
Onomatopoeic Adverbs	159
Onushi	13
Or	163
Ordinal Numbers	39
Ore	11
Order of Words	182
Ordinal Numbers	39

	Page
Oru	55, 110
Other People	32
Ought	163
Parts of Speech	5
Particles, Order of	183
Passive Verbs	83
Past Participle	53
Past Tense	55
Perfect Future	59
Personal Pronoun	11
Please	180
Plural	7
Possessive Pronoun	16
Potential Verbs	79
Predicate	94
Prepositions	159
Present Indicative	71
Probable Past	59
Pronoun	11
,, limited use of	15
Pronunciation	3
Ra	7, 19, 141, 173
Rashi	101
Reflexive Pronouns	30
Relations	167
Relative Pronouns	30
Riōhō	33
Ro	75
Sa (Abstract Terms)	101
Sa (that)	21
Sa (Particle.)	141
Sahodo	18
San or Sama	173
Saseru	81
Self	30
Sensei	13
Seru	81
Sessha	11
She	14

INDEX.

	Page
Shi	100, 142
Shika	18
Shinjô	191
Shiu	164
Should	7, 143, 173
Sochi	13, 18
Sochira	19
Soitsu	18
Sokka	13
Soko	18
Sokora	19
Somebody	29
Something	29
So	21
Sonata	18, 23
Sonna	21
Sonnani	18
Sono	21
Sono hô	13
Sore	21
Stems, as Nouns	10
„ of Verbs	50
„ of Adj.	94
Su	81
Superficial or Land Measure.	189
Suru with uninflected Words	85
„ Conjugation	46, 48
„ with Negatives	51
„ to do	111
Ta	55
Tachi	7, 143, 173
Tagai ni	31
Tai	61, 102
Takke	57
Tara	57
Taraba	57
Tareba	57
Taredo	61
Tari	60

	Page
Tarô	59
Taru	55
Te (with Adj.)	96
Te (Past Participle)	53
Temaye	11, 13
Te mo	97
Terminations of Verbs	186
Te wa with Adj.	97
„ „ with Verbs	55
That	18, 21, 25, 164
They	14
Theirs	16
Think	164
This	18, 19
Though	161
Time	186
To	144, 164
Tokoro	32, 106, 125
Tōnin	14
Transitive and Intransitive Verbs	78
Uninflected Words	6
„ used as Adjectives.	104
Unu	13
Verbs	42
Verbal Form of Adj.	100
Wa	148
Waga	30
Want	165
Ware	13
Washi	11
Watai	11
Watakŭshi	11, 15
Watashi	11
Wattchi	11
We	11, 15
Week	188
Weights	190
What	27

INDEX.

	Page		Page
When	.. 33	Years	.. 186
Who	18, 25	Yo	75, 154
Why	18, 27	Yori	.. 155
Wo	.. 151	You	12, 13
Would	.. 165	Yours	.. 16
Ya	.. 152	Zo	.. 155
Yara	.. 153	Zu	.. 66
Ye	.. 153	Zuba	.. 66

ERRATUM.

Bottom of p. 57 after *tabetareba*, add *kashitaraba*, *tabetaraba*.

Printed at the "*Hakubunsha*" *Tokio.*

www.ingramcontent.com/pod-product-compliance
Lightning Source LLC
Chambersburg PA
CBHW031827230426
43669CB00009B/1251